practicing your path

a book of retreats for an intentional life

by holly w. whitcomb

innisfree press, inc.
philadelphia, pennsylvania

PRACTICING YOUR PATH
A Book of Retreats for an Intentional Life

Large-quantity purchases or custom editions of this book are available at a discount from the publisher. For more information, contact the sales department at Augsburg Fortress, Publishers, 1-800-328-4648, or write to: Sales Director, Augsburg Fortress, Publishers, Box 1209, Minneapolis, MN 55440-1209.

Unless otherwise indicated, Scripture passages are from the New Revised Standard Version of the Bible, copyright © 1946, 1952, 1971, 1989 by the Division of Christian Education of the National Council of the Churches of Christ in the USA. Used by permission.

Cover photo © Daisuke Monita/Photodisc Red/Getty Images. Used by permission.

The paper used in this publication meets the minimum requirements of American National Standard for Information Sciences—Permanence of Paper for Printed Library Materials, ANSI Z329.48-1984.

Manufactured in the U.S.A.

The author gratefully acknowledges permission to reprint the following excerpts:

From *Feasting with God: Adventures in Table Spirituality* by Holly W. Whitcomb. (Cleveland: United Church Press, 1996), 45-46, 142. Copyright © 1996. Used by permission.

From *Let Your Life Speak: Listening for the Voice of Vocation* by Parker J. Palmer, Copyright © 2000 by Jossey-Bass, Inc., Publishers. Reprinted by permission of John Wiley & Sons, inc.

The English translation of the "Magnificat" (Canticle of Mary) from *The Liturgical Psalter* © 1995, International Committee on English in the Liturgy, Inc. All rights reserved. Reprinted by permission.

From *Oblique Prayers* by Denise Levertov, copyright © 1984 by Denise Levertov. Reprinted by permission of New Directions Publishing Corp. and Pollinger, Ltd.

From *A Path with Heart* by Jack Kornfield, copyright © 1993 by Jack Kornfield. Used by permission of Bantam Books, a division of Random House, Inc.

Portions of this book have appeared as follows in previously published pieces:

A version of "Sabbath: A Space for Grace" (in chapter 1) first appeared in *Re-Imagining: Quarterly Publications of the Re-Imagining Community 25* (November 2000): 22-23.

A version of "A Letter about Sabbath" (in chapter 1) first appeared as "The Spaciousness of Sabbath: A Correspondence" in *Spirit Unfolding: Newsletter of the Spiritual Development Network of the United Church of Christ* (Summer 2000): 1-2. Reprinted with permission.

A version of "On Loan to Love" (in chapter 5) first appeared in *No Other Foundation* (Wisconsin Conference of the United Church of Christ) 15, number 1 (Summer 1994): 49-52.

A version of "What Is a Spiritual Director?" (in chapter 7) first appeared in *Re-Imagining: Quarterly Publication of the Re-Imagining Community 25* (November 2000): 23.

Versions of the discussion of "A Daily Inventory or Examination of Conscience" (in chapter 7) first appeared as "Daily Inventory" in *Praying: Spirituality for Everyday Living* 90 (January 15, 1999): 33-34 and in *Ordinary Ministry, Extraordinary Challenge: Women and the Roles of Ministry,* edited by Norma Cook Everist (Nashville: Abingdon, 2000), 38-39. Adapted by permission.

A shorter version of this book was published as *The Bible and Spiritual Disciplines: Insights, Bible Studies for Growing Faith* (Cleveland: United Church Press, 2000). Used by permission.

In memory of my dad,
in thanksgiving for his fanciful imagination
and his inventive spirit

 contents

 # acknowledgments

Thank you . . .

sister, Heather, for always listening eagerly
to any aspect of my creative progress

manuscript readers Bonnie Andrews and Rita Sorensen
for offering their time, encouragement and astute critique

my publisher and editor, Marcia Broucek, who understood better than I
how this book should look in final form

writing industry expert Carolyn Kott Washburne for her marketing advice

friend and creative companion Nancy Vollbrecht for always asking the question:
How is God nurturing your creativity right now?

walking buddy and confidante Kathleen Adams for all of our miles
pounding the pavement together and for "hearing each other into speech"
(Nelle Morton's concept from *The Journey Is Home*)

dear friend and muse Agnes Barrett for always watching out for me

Brookfield Public Library for comfortable and secret writing places

the members of the staff of the Elm Grove Public Library
who never fail to get me any book my heart desires—one way or another

all of my retreatants and spiritual direction seekers
who inspire and teach me as they practice their paths in wisdom and faith

my husband, John, our son, David, and our daughter, Kate,
who love me and cajole me and like my food

 # introduction

I love walking. It has not always been so. The more I've done it, the easier it has become. Now I really look forward to putting on my walking shoes and stepping out. I depend on walking to keep me sane and lovable. Walking offers me muscle tone and inner space. Walking offers me robust energy and time to think. I'm pretty good at walking by myself, but sometimes it's rainy and dreary. Sometimes it's hard to make the effort to change clothes. Sometimes I'm just too tired and feel like napping instead.

In the last two years I've joined a hiking club. I still walk a lot of miles by myself, but I'm also relishing the camaraderie of walking with other people. I like to know there are others also paying close attention to our natural surroundings: that cedar waxwing sitting over there on the branch, that dinner-plate dahlia sending vibrant color into a corner garden, that ruffle-barked burr oak struggling to grow along that busy road.

Most importantly, however, my fellow hikers never cancel. They show up in the rain. They show up in the hail. They show up if it's a muggy one hundred degrees. Their energy and commitment help me to show up, too.

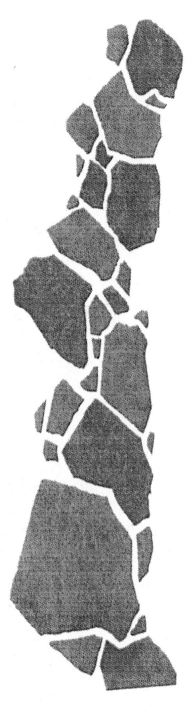

Perhaps our physical paths and our spiritual paths are not so different one from the other. We do not just slip into a satisfying spiritual life. We practice it. We practice it again and again and again. We can grow enormously by practicing alone, but it also helps to have others show up to pay attention with us. It is a delight to share the motivation and inspiration of companions: to benefit from their joys, their struggles, their empathy, and their support.

This book, *Practicing Your Path*, explores seven pivotal components of classical Christian spirituality: the practice of Sabbath, the practice of hospitality, the practice of intercessory prayer, the practice of fasting, the practice of stewardship, the practice of living into your call, and the practice of accountability. If we learn to live into these seven spiritual practices, we can live a life of integrity and fruitfulness.

These seven retreats can stand alone or can be used in conjunction with any or all of the others. *Practicing Your Path* is presented in the author's favorite order, but there is no correct sequence. Examine the topics and see what would work best for you. Perhaps you could do a retreat every several months. Or you might select some of them for a special time period, such as Lent or as a part of a church group series. In Appendix A, after the last retreat, there is an optional "End-of-Series Celebration" that you may want to include as part of your last retreat.

You may choose to go on retreat with this book by yourself and you will reap benefits. You will probably gain even more if you plan these retreats with a faith community and explore your spiritual lives together. It is a rare privilege to experience the intimacy and trust of practicing a spiritual path with others.

May God bless you as you practice your own path, in whatever way is right for you. May God bless all of us as we practice our paths together and try to live an intentional life.

preface

 *How to Use this Book if You're Retreating Alone*

SUGGESTION ONE: The principal advantage of going on retreat is the gaining of perspective. Perspective offers us wisdom and discernment. When you decide to take a day of retreat, give yourself at least a whole day. Don't plan one of these retreats between a morning appointment and an evening meeting. Turn off all your phones. Transform your whole day into what theologian Maria Harris would call a day of "deep listening." If you can, get out of your house or out of town. Go to a retreat center or a campground or a church or a friend's house. Go somewhere peaceful where you won't be sucked into obligations and responsibilities.

SUGGESTION TWO: Be flexible. Adjust your time, taking breaks as you need. If you like some of the suggested activities and don't like others, do what appeals to you. You know your needs better than anyone else. And don't worry if you fall asleep. Take a long nap if you like. Most of all, take your time and practice *being* instead of *doing.*

SUGGESTION THREE: The retreats contain some "art as meditation" exercises. Play with them. The emphasis is on process, not on product. This is not a contest. Creative expression can help you to get out of your head, into your heart. Be open.

How to Use this Book if You're Retreating with a Group

These retreats are appropriate for whole congregations, several congregations together, church councils, women's groups, men's groups, spiritual seekers' groups, just about any gathering of adults from the Christian tradition seeking a spiritual deepening.

If you are the retreat leader, adapt these retreats for your own purposes. *Suggestions for group use are given in the margins throughout,* but feel free to adapt them to meet your group's needs. Think about the members of your group and what content and time frame works best for them. Will your retreat be a day-long experience? A retreat from 9:30 A.M. until 3:30 P.M. works especially well, giving participants time to eat breakfast with their families and still get home before dinner. Will your retreat be an overnight and a day long? Starting at 7:00 P.M. on Friday and going until 3:00 or 4:00 P.M. on Saturday gives the participants a little re-entry time late Saturday afternoon. Will your retreat be a weekend retreat? Try Friday at 7:00 P.M. through noon (before or after lunch) on Sunday. If your retreat starts Friday and ends Sunday, a change of pace works well for Saturday night, perhaps a sing-along, a drama, a movie, a talent show, or some other kind of creative sharing. If your retreat is over a weekend, build in some worship time together on Sunday morning.

Sit down ahead of time with the retreat material and decide what to use. Meet with your planning committee, if you are working with a larger group. Think about the suggestions and pray about them. Look over all the material, including the part marked "To Plan a Longer Retreat." Pick and choose the parts you think would work well for your group. Although some song suggestions are given, choose songs people in your retreat will know.

Be sure to allow enough spiritual space. (There is nothing worse than a retreat that seems like another overcrowded business meeting!) The length of the morning retreat times and afternoon retreat times are only suggestions. Look around. Pay attention to your participants. Adjust the time, taking breaks as people need. Be flexible. Create. Adapt. Revise. You know your participants better than anyone else. Make this work for them. Plan ahead for any props, handouts, music, or art supplies you need to bring.

Don't worry if you don't get to everything you had planned. It is much better to stay loose and to let people have time than to inflict an artificial agenda that makes everyone feel exhausted and controlled. Have confidence in your own judgment and trust God's spirit to move.

Relax. Enjoy. Practice your path. Trust God to show you the way.

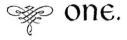 # one.

practicing sabbath

transforming human doing into human being

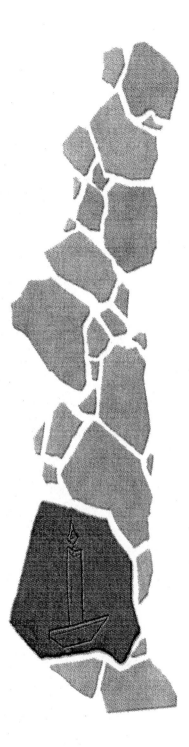

When we are capable of stopping, we begin to see and, if we can see, we understand. . . . We should master the art of stopping in order to really be . . .[1]
—Thich Nhat Hanh, *Peace Is Every Step*

One of the astonishing attributes of Sabbath time is its unflinching uselessness.[2]
—Wayne Muller, *Sabbath*

theme

This retreat is about Sabbath-keeping: learning what Sabbath is, exploring why it is vital to your spiritual life, and discovering creative and sustaining ways to observe it.

planning ahead

One week before your day of retreat, read Exodus 20:8-11. Ponder the following questions for reflection and let them simmer as you go about your daily activities:

What does Sabbath mean to you?
How do you observe Sabbath?
What happens when you take Sabbath time?

Before your retreat day, collect the following materials, so you won't be distracted during your retreat:

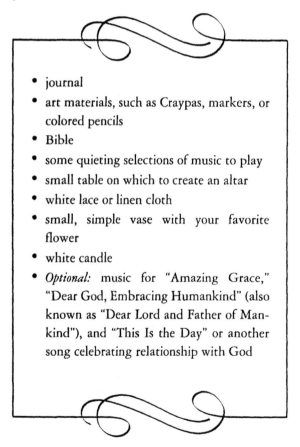

- journal
- art materials, such as Craypas, markers, or colored pencils
- Bible
- some quieting selections of music to play
- small table on which to create an altar
- white lace or linen cloth
- small, simple vase with your favorite flower
- white candle
- *Optional:* music for "Amazing Grace," "Dear God, Embracing Humankind" (also known as "Dear Lord and Father of Mankind"), and "This Is the Day" or another song celebrating relationship with God

If you are doing this retreat with a group . . .

Leader: *Reflect on this scripture and these questions for your own preparation. Pray for yourself and each retreat participant.*

Leader: *In addition to asking people to bring a journal and a Bible, you will need to supply some art materials. Also, an easel with newsprint and markers is helpful.*

CREATING SACRED SPACE

Create an altar by covering a small table with an old-fashioned white lace or linen cloth. Place on the cloth one flower in a small, simple vase and light a white candle.

MORNING (2 - 2 ½ HOURS)

welcome

Welcome this new day. Stretch your arms toward the sky, inhaling deeply your hopes for this day, exhaling whatever anxieties you wish to put aside. After repeating this several times, consider singing or playing a favorite piece of music to quiet your heart.

Leader: *After leading the group in some stretching and breathing, your welcome should include a description of the day's theme. Suggest a song for the group to sing together or play a quieting piece of music.*

CENTERING

Sit for a few minutes in silence with your hands open on your lap, receptive to God's leading. Prayerfully ponder and review the distractions or obstacles that may be blocking you from receiving this retreat fully. Pass these over to God's loving care. Sit for a few minutes in silence and offer a prayer of invocation asking God's blessing on your retreat.

Leader: *After this time of centering and prayer, allow some time for introductions. If the group is less than twenty, go around the circle answering the question: "Is there anything you remember learning about Sabbath as a child?" If the group is larger, have people share in smaller groups. (See Appendix B for other Welcoming Suggestions.)*

SCRIPTURE

Read Exodus 20:8-11.

Remember the sabbath day, and keep it holy. Six days you shall labor and do all your work. But the seventh day is a sabbath to the LORD your God; you shall not do any work—you, your son or your daughter, your male or female slave, your livestock, or the alien resident in your towns. For in six days the LORD made heaven and earth, the sea, and all that is in them, but rested the seventh day; therefore the LORD blessed the sabbath day and consecrated it.

meditation

Keeping the Sabbath

Stay still for a while.
Listen.
Where am I today?
How is God moving in my life?

Leader: *Present this material in a way that is comfortable for you. Adapt this meditation any way you like, or create your own.*

If I were asked to name the two most necessary components of my spiritual life, I would instantly reply, "prayer and Sabbath." I cannot imagine navigating my everyday existence without these two. When I was young, I believed that Sabbath was an unproductive waste of time: good works and hard work seemed to be more effective and more laudable. Now in my middle age, when the quickly evident fruits of non-Sabbath appear in the form of witheredness, weariness, and despair, I am newly in love with the necessity of Sabbath. The motto of Outward Bound reminds me, "If you can't get out of it, get into it!" That's how I feel about Sabbath. For years, to my own detriment, I have tried to get out of Sabbath, so now I'm getting into it and thriving.

Sabbath is a time of deep listening, of rest, of doing nothing—no thing. It is an opportunity to reconnect with ourselves and with our God. There are no shoulds or oughts in Sabbath. It is a time that exists only for itself, a time of being, rather than doing.

Tilden Edwards writes:

Not long ago the religion instructor at a Christian high school decided to introduce silent meditation into one of his classes. He gave the students instructions simply to "be" during the silence: to be relaxed and awake, open to life as it is, with nothing to do but appreciate whatever comes. Week by week he slowly increased the amount of time to a maximum of ten minutes.

The student response was very revealing. One boy summarized a general feeling of the class: "It is the only time in my day when I am not expected to achieve something." The response of several irate parents was equally revealing: "It isn't Christian," said one. "I'm not paying all that tuition for my child to sit there and do nothing," proclaimed another.

How is it that ten minutes of silence can be so special and so threatening?[3]

Think about the young boy's response: "It is the only time in my day when I am not expected to achieve something." This statement alone is the essence of Sabbath. Sabbath is not about achievement. It is about being.

The commandment to observe Sabbath stems from the Ten Commandments found in the books of Exodus and Deuteronomy. (Yes, it really is in there with the rest of the Ten Commandments. Why do we remember the ones about adultery and covetousness and murder better than this one?)

Orthodox Jews know more about honoring this sense of being rather than doing than we do as Christians. To the Jews, all the rest of the week culminates in the richness and renewal of the Sabbath from sundown Friday until sundown on Saturday. Sabbath is not an afterthought, but the crown, the pinnacle of creation. Sabbath teaches both Jews and Christians a rhythm between being versus doing, grace versus drivenness, rest versus work. If we listen, Sabbath teaches us that our identity does not have to be earned; it is given from God. It is through Sabbath that grace and freedom are restored.

But the question remains, how do we go about observing Sabbath? Traditionally Sabbath in the Christian tradition is Sunday. You may have been practicing a faithful and heartfelt Sabbath time for years. And for some, Sunday worship and Sunday rest remain gratifying Sabbath experiences. Unfortunately for many others of us, clergy or lay, Sunday is a day filled with church business, church responsibilities, or church distractions. For thousands of people, Sunday is simply another day to show up at work.

So it is up to us to live into the commandment to observe the Sabbath faithfully and to find Sabbath somehow and somewhere.

Only you, in your heart, know what the best Sabbath time is for you. For one person, the best Sabbath time may be a long, hot bath each evening. For another person, Sabbath may mean gathering around the table for a weekly meal with good friends. For another, Sabbath may be a daily devotional time in the morning, or perhaps an afternoon time digging in the garden. For others, Sabbath may be a time of walking, reading, or singing. Donna Schaper in her book *Sabbath Sense* calls it "spiritual leisure,"[4] "a turn in the road back to grace."[5] I especially like this image. It makes the dictionary definition of grace as "the influence or spirit of God operating in humans to regenerate or strengthen them"[6] come alive.

Whatever Sabbath is, I like to call it an intentional time and space for God to enter in. Sabbath is a time of re-creation, a time of remembering who and whose we are.

MORNING REFLECTION
(allow about an hour for this)

Gather your journal and some art materials, and settle into a comfortable place where you can reflect on these questions and record your thoughts and feelings.

1. In her book *Sabbath Sense* Donna Schaper says that Sabbath means:

- humans, being.
- no shoulds.
- putting margins on the pages of our days.
- standing and being still, long enough, that we see into the depth of time.
- our relief. It is our way out of urgency. It is the turn in the road back to grace.[7]

Which of these statements about Sabbath makes the most sense to you?

Leader: *Have the journaling questions written on newsprint ahead of time so people can copy them into their journals (or have them printed on handouts). Direct people to take their journals to a place where they can quietly respond to the questions. Let them know they will have 40 minutes. Then gather everyone back together by singing "Amazing Grace." Divide people into groups of 5, counting off by the letters G-R-A-C-E, if the numbers come out right. Invite them to share for 20 minutes what is comfortable from their journaling and drawing.*

2. Sing the song "Amazing Grace" to yourself, paying particular attention to the words. What is grace for you? How do you experience it?

3. Using your art materials, draw an image of grace. There is no wrong way or right way to do this. Think of creating a visual image as a helpful way to see or understand something that you didn't know before. How does this image speak to you? Meditate on what you have created.

sabbath breathing and sabbath singing

Sabbath Breathing

. . . in the book of Exodus we read, "In six days God made heaven and earth, and on the seventh day God rested, and was refreshed." Here the word "refreshed," vaiynafesh, *literally means "and God exhaled." The creation of the world was like the life-quickening inhale. The Sabbath is the exhale. Thus . . . all creation moves with the rhythm of the inhale and the exhale. Without the Sabbath exhale, the life-giving inhale is impossible.[8]*
—Wayne Muller, *Sabbath*

Relax. Get comfortable. Sit and breathe. In and out. Breathe in creativity. Breathe out Sabbath. Breathe in creativity. Breathe out Sabbath. Do this five times. Remember that Sabbath is the exhale.

Sabbath Singing

Sing or read aloud a song of Sabbath, such as the following three verses of "Dear God, Embracing Humankind," (also known as "Dear Lord and Father of Mankind"). Note this: The melody is called "Rest."

O sabbath rest by Galilee!
O calm of hills above!
There Jesus met you prayerfully;
the silence of eternity,
interpreted by love.

Drop your still dews of quietness,
till all our strivings cease;
Take from our souls the strain and stress,
and let our ordered lives confess
the beauty of your peace.

Breathe through the pulses of desire
your coolness and your balm;
Let sense be numb,
let flesh retire;
speak through the earthquake, wind, and fire,
O still, small voice of calm.[9]

A PRAYER BEFORE EATING

Gracious God, for work I give thanks.
Gracious God, for play I give thanks.
Gracious God, for rest I give thanks.
Gracious God, for food I give thanks. Amen.

Leader: *Write the prayer on newsprint or have the participants repeat each line after you. Change the "I" to "we." Stand and hold hands in a circle.*

lunch and free time (2 hours)

Optional question to ponder during free time:

> *How am I observing Sabbath?*

If possible, walk outside, absorb the season, notice nature. If you can't go outside, consider relaxing with a new symbol or a new posture. Maybe you could sit in front of a lighted candle or lie on your back on the floor with your arms and legs extended.

afternoon (1 ½ to 2 hours)

centering

Sing a song such as "This Is the Day" or another song celebrating relationship with God. Or, you may want to sit with your palms open in a spirit of receptivity.

meditation

Leader: *Present this material in a way that is comfortable for you. One possibility is to read this letter aloud or ask a volunteer to read it.*

A Letter About Sabbath [10]

Dear Elizabeth,

I was delighted to receive your letter. With summer coming upon us, how fitting it is that you should find yourself ruminating about rest and renewal. Let me respond by talking about Sabbath. I am crazy about Sabbath! I have lived for decades as a driven, frantic person, and it has only been recently through the consistent observing of Sabbath that I have regained a healthy perspective. A couple of years ago, a colleague looked me in the eye and said, "Tell me about your day off." I hemmed and hawed for a while and then admitted that there was no day off.

"Why isn't there a day off?" she asked. My answer revealed a lot. It turned out I didn't think I deserved one. And why didn't I think I deserved one? Because all my worth was wrapped up in what I could achieve.

This attitude, I suppose, is the antithesis of Sabbath. Sabbath talks about being rather than doing. Sabbath talks about rest rather than work. For years, I was exhausted and cynical. Sabbath has given me back my life. I have learned that being faithful to Sabbath-keeping means being loved just as one is. Ironically, when I keep Sabbath faithfully, I also end up feeling energized and purposeful and connected. I confess with a considerable amount of embarrassment that I no longer feel I am indispensable. Imagine. What a gift that has been!

There is no way any of us is going to enter into Sabbath until we push our large or small egos out of the way and say, "I want to get to know and love God. I want to get to know and love the me that is separate from my work. I want to say thank you for the real me that God loves just as is, no qualifiers attached."

It has taken me a few years to appreciate fully the fruits of my Sabbath. Now if I don't experience those fruits on a weekly basis, I become crabby and diminished and hard to live with. Monday is my Sabbath Day, and on Mondays I spring out of bed. There are no shoulds or oughts on that day. On Mondays, I do the things I love. I may begin the day with a long walk and perhaps some prayer. There is almost always a trip to one bead shop or another. My hobby is jewelry-making, and I love to wander around the bead stores looking at the colorful trays, fantasizing about what I'm going to put together next. Then I often have lunch with one friend or another and catch up on news and laugh a lot. Frequently Monday is a letter-writing day, not because I have to but because I enjoy writing letters. Letter-writing is a way of building community for me, a way of tending relationships, a way of telling my loved ones that they are important. Maybe I'll take a two-hour nap. Sometimes I'll cook on Mondays, too, perhaps taking time to make a more intricate and rewarding recipe than usual, one that deserves leisure time. I am usually a bit wistful on Monday night that the day is almost over, but then I thank God that I finally discovered what a good Sabbath day can be. On Tuesday I'm ready to go back to work because I have been given the spaciousness I needed. I have been refueled. I have been reconnected. I have been reminded that I am much more than my work. Sabbath offers me a larger picture. Observing Sabbath helps me to lighten up and to breathe.

You asked me about vacation. We're all planning our vacations with the summer months approaching. Is vacation the same as Sabbath time? That's something to think about, isn't it? The word "vacation" is from the Latin *vacatio*, which means "freedom from something." Vacation can certainly be Sabbath if it is rest, if it is spacious, if it is not filled with shoulds or oughts. But many of us go on vacation as frenetically as we go to work each morning, and that is not a pretty sight. When we go on vacation, it may be helpful to ask ourselves: Are we truly experiencing "freedom from something" or are we experiencing bondage to everything? Is our vacation time filled with obligations and expectations and agendas that are packed way too tightly? How can we plan vacations that don't leave us feeling more fatigued and over-stimulated than when we left? This is certainly something to consider if we're going to think about what Sabbath means to our lives.

I love Sabbath. I know that now there is no way I could live without it. Tilden Edwards calls it "the eternal rhythm." Rabbi Abraham Joshua Heschel calls it " a sanctuary—a cathedral in time." Whatever Sabbath is, it is a time to remember that we are unconditionally loved and that we are held by the grace of God.

This poem, "The Avowal" by Denise Levertov (*Oblique Prayers*) sums up Sabbath for me:

> *As swimmers dare*
> *to lie face to the sky*
> *and water bears them,*
> *as hawks rest upon air*
> *and air sustains them,*
> *so would I learn to attain*
> *free-fall, and float*
> *into Creator Spirit's deep embrace,*
> *knowing no effort earns*
> *that all-surrounding grace.*[11]

I'll talk to you soon. Have a good restful summer.

Warmly,
Holly

song

Sing the song "This Is <u>My</u> Day" once again, this time substituting "my" for "the" and changing the words all the way through: "I will rejoice," etc.[12] Or sing another song celebrating relationship with God

afternoon reflection

(allow about an hour)

Gather your journal and some art materials, and settle into a comfortable place where you can reflect on these questions and record your thoughts and feelings.

1. What did you hear in the meditation letter about Sabbath? What emotions of your own were expressed? Which part, if any, seemed to be written to you?

2. Sabbath can be observed in solitude, such as taking a walk alone. Sabbath can also be observed in community, by worshiping in church or sharing a meal. Do you observe Sabbath in solitude or in community or in both ways?

3. If Sabbath is "an intentional time and space for God to enter in" or "spiritual leisure," where are you finding and observing Sabbath in your life right now?

4. Are there any new ways in which you would like to be observing Sabbath?

Leader: *Have the journaling questions written on newsprint ahead of time so people can copy them into their journals (or have them printed on handouts). Direct people to take their journals and some art materials to a place where they can quietly respond to the questions. Let them know they will have 40 minutes. Then gather everyone back together by singing a song, if you wish. Divide people into groups of 4, counting off by the letters T-I-M-E, if the numbers come out right. Invite them to share for 20 minutes what is comfortable from their journaling and drawing.*

5. Draw an image, or illustrate a set of words, of what a Sabbath time might look like for you. As you reflect on your image, consider what kind of commitment you want to make to increase your Sabbath time. Who in your life could offer you Sabbath-keeping support?

closing ritual

SABBATH POSSIBILITIES: As your Sabbath retreat comes to a close, sit quietly in front of your altar table and let the candlelight bring your thoughts into focus. With your palms open, ponder your Sabbath possibilities.

SONG: Sing this old Song of Sabbath to the tune of "Amazing Grace." (The words for this Sabbath song were written by John Ellerton who was born in 1826.)

Behold us, God, a little space
From daily tasks set free,
And met within thy holy place
To rest awhile with thee.

Around us rolls the ceaseless tide
Of business, toil, and care,
And scarcely can we turn aside
For one brief hour of prayer.[13]

Leader: *Ask participants to stand quietly in a circle pondering their Sabbath possibilities. (Observe a minute of silence.) Pass around the circle a gesture of kindness: Take the next person's hands in both of your own and wish them the traditional Jewish Sabbath greeting, "Shabbat shalom, sabbath peace." Pass this gesture and greeting from one to another until everyone has received it.*

Making Room for God

Create a new retreat called "Making Room for God" by combining this "Practicing Sabbath" retreat and the "Practicing the Fast" retreat on page 53 together into one longer weekend retreat. The theme of the new retreat could be described in the following way.

THEME: This retreat challenges us to think about how we go about making room for God in our busy lives. It focuses on inviting God to act in our lives through (1) our observance of Sabbath, and (2) our practice of relinquishment: taking a good look at those things that we do to excess and that keep God at a distance.

 ## two.

practicing hospitality

creating welcome space
for god,
for self,
for others

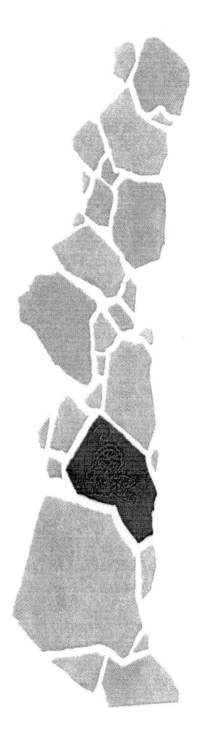

Do not neglect to show hospitality to strangers, for by doing that some have entertained angels without knowing it.
—Hebrews 13:2

theme

This retreat will help you take a fresh look at the grace-filled and respectful practice of hospitality as you ask yourself: How can I be more hospitable to God, to myself, to others?

planning ahead

One week before your day of retreat, write your own definition of hospitality. Ask yourself the question,

How has God been hospitable to me?

Make a list and let these ideas simmer as you go about your daily activities.

Before your retreat day, collect the following materials, so you won't be distracted during your retreat:

- journal
- art materials, such as Craypas, markers, or colored pencils
- Bible
- some quieting selections of music to play
- small table on which to create an altar
- cornucopia or attractive basket
- flowers, fruits or vegetables (whatever is currently being harvested) to fill your cornucopia
- votive candles in small glass cups
- *Optional:* music for two songs about God's hospitality, such as "Joyful, Joyful, We Adore Thee"; music for "Blessed Be the Tie That Binds"
- *For longer retreats:* a blank index or recipe card.

If you are doing this retreat with a group . . .

Leader: *Write this definition and make this list for your own preparation. Spend some time with the questions on page 36 about hospitality to God, to self, and to others. Pray for yourself and each retreat participant.*

Leader: *In addition to asking people bring a journal and a Bible, you will need to supply some art materials. Also, an easel with newsprint and markers is helpful. (If you're going to do the longer retreat, bring blank index or recipe cards for each participant, along with a small box, such as a recipe box, in which to collect the cards.)*

CREATING SACRED SPACE

Create an altar table as a colorful and welcoming focal point. Make a centerpiece with a cornucopia or basket filled with the flowers, fruits, or vegetables you have gathered. Surround it with lighted votive candles in small glass cups.

MORNING (2 to 2 ½ hours)

WELCOME

Welcome this new day. Stretch your arms toward the sky, inhaling deeply your hopes for this day, exhaling whatever anxieties you wish to put aside. After repeating this several times, consider singing or playing a favorite piece of music to quiet your heart.

Leader: *After leading the group in some stretching and breathing, your welcome should include a description of the day's theme. Suggest a song for the group to sing together or play a quieting piece of music.*

CENTERING

Sit for a few minutes in silence with your hands open on your lap, receptive to God's leading. Breathe in welcome. Breathe out suspicion. Repeat this several times. Prayerfully ponder and review the distractions or obstacles that may be blocking you from receiving this retreat fully. Pass these over to God's loving care. Sit for a few minutes in silence and offer a prayer of invocation asking God's blessing on your retreat.

Leader: *After this time of centering and prayer, allow some time for introductions. If the group is less than twenty, go around the circle answering the question: "What scenario comes to mind first when you recall being treated with extraordinary hospitality?" If the group is larger, have people share in smaller groups. (See Appendix B for other Welcoming Suggestions.)*

JOURNALING TIME (allow about 15 minutes)

Use the following questions to guide your reflections. Record your thoughts and feelings in your journal.

1. What do you think of when you hear the word "hospitality"?

2. Are there any Bible stories that immediately come to mind when you hear the word "hospitality"?

3. From what you read in the Bible, how does Jesus exhibit hospitality?

4. In what ways has God provided hospitality to you?

SCRIPTURE

Read James 2:14-17.

MEDITATION

What is Hospitality?

I love to visit my good friend Oleta in Albuquerque, New Mexico, because she serves up hospitality with kindness and panache. She meets me, smiling and enthusiastic, at the airport gate as I get off my plane. She drives me to her house, ushers me to a lovely guestroom filled with windows, books, a cozy reading light, walls full of art, and a fluffy, warm bed opulent with soft pillows and extra blankets. After I use the fresh towels she has laid out in a bathroom filled with fresh flowers, she summons me to eat an exotic and delicious Southwestern dinner. (Aren't all meals prepared by another exotic and delicious?) And then she asks: "How are you? What's going on in your life? How is your family? How are you feeling creative and alive these days?"

Leader: *Write these questions on newsprint and, instead of journaling, discuss with the whole group.*

Leader: *Present this material in a way that is comfortable for you. Adapt this meditation any way you like, or create your own.*

My body is refreshed. My soul sings. My physical and emotional needs are tended. I am accepted, respected, cared for. My welcome is abundant.

The word "hospitality" comes from the Greek *hospes,* which means a host or a guest. Isn't it interesting that the Greek word *hospes* means BOTH host and guest? When we're welcoming guests into our home, we ourselves as the hosts often end up benefitting most from that relationship. Isn't it ironic that it is often the guest who brings refreshment or newness or stimulation and ends up offering hospitality to the host? The dictionary describes hospitality as the act, practice, or quality of receiving and entertaining strangers or guests in a friendly and generous way.

In biblical times, hospitality was regarded as a law, a holy duty. First Peter 4:9 says "Be hospitable to one another without complaining." Romans 12:13 says "Contribute to the needs of the saints, practice hospitality" (*RSV*). In James 2:14-17 is found perhaps the strongest of all the admonitions to hospitality:

> What good is it my brothers and sisters, if you say you have faith but do not have works? Can faith save you? If a brother or sister is naked and lacks daily food, and one of you says to them, "Go in peace; keep warm and eat your fill," and yet you do not supply their bodily needs, what is the good of that? So faith by itself, if it has no works, is dead.

In speaking of the age-old biblical tradition of hospitality, theologian Marjorie Thompson writes:

> It is hard for us to comprehend, but hospitality in the ancient Near East was originally offered to complete strangers. People who appeared from the unknown might bear gifts or might be enemies. Because travel was a dangerous venture, codes of hospitality were strict. If a sworn enemy showed up at your doorstep asking for food and shelter, you were bound to supply his request, along with protection and safe passage as long as he was on your land. All sorts of people had to travel at times through "enemy territory," which meant that hospitality to strangers was a matter of mutual survival. It was a kind of social covenant, an implied commitment to transcend human differences in order to meet common human needs.[14]

Inspired by the remarkable hospitality of the Jews, who realized that all people were once strangers in a strange land somewhere, the early Christian community was known for its hospitality: its inclusive care for all, regardless of social status. In the midst of Roman society, the Christian community was known by its concern for the newly arrived, the poor, the elderly, those in prison, the disabled, all the disenfranchised. One Roman emperor ordered his provincial governors to exhibit hospitality like that of the Christians.

In our busy, modern society, we have lost touch with that ancient, grace-filled, and respectful practice of hospitality, that holy duty which provides an unconditional welcome to stranger or guest or outcast. We need to reclaim the presence of hospitality in all aspects of our lives. We need to invite hospitality to heal us as we become mindful of all those whom we could be inviting in. In the fifth century, St. Benedict coined a classic expression of hospitality: "All guests . . . are to be welcomed as Christ, for he himself will say: *I was a stranger and you welcomed me* (Matthew 25:35)."[15]

SONG

If you wish, sing a song about God's hospitality, such as "Joyful, Joyful, We Adore Thee."

BIBLE STUDY (allow about 45 minutes)

Choose three of the following scriptures you feel drawn to. Take your time to prayerfully read the three you have chosen. Do not rush.

- I Kings 17:8-16:
  Elijah and the Widow of Zarephath

- Luke 19:1-10:
  Jesus and Zaccheus

- Genesis 18:1-15:
  Three angels with Abraham and Sarah

- Matthew 25:31-46:
  Christ in the guise of the stranger

- Luke 10:38-42:
  Jesus and Mary and Martha

Leader: *Divide the larger group into five small groups. Assign one Bible passage to each and ask for a volunteer note-taker from each group. Write these instructions:*

- *Have someone read the passage slowly aloud.*

- *Sit in silence for about three minutes meditating on the passage.*

- *What does this passage tell you about hospitality? Discuss.*

- *How does this passage inspire you to act in your own life? Discuss.*

Give the groups about 30 minutes for their reading and discussion. Then call the groups back together and have the note-taker summarize how their particular scripture spoke to their group.

Use your journal to record your thoughts and feelings about what you have read.

1. What does each passage say about hospitality?
2. How does each passage inspire you to act in your life?

INTERLUDE

Sit quietly and give thanks for all the hospitality that has come your way.

Leader: *Choose a song to sing together before lunch, if you wish.*

A PRAYER BEFORE EATING
(A REMINDER OF GOD'S HOSPITALITY TO US)

> In this food,
> I see clearly the presence
> of the entire universe
> supporting my existence.[16]
> Amen.

Leader: *Write this prayer on newsprint so that all may pray it together. Stand and hold hands in a circle.*

LUNCH AND FREE TIME (2 HOURS)

Optional question to ponder during free time:

> How am I extending hospitality
> to God, myself, and others?

If possible, walk outside, absorb the season, notice nature. If you can't go outside, consider relaxing with a new symbol or a new posture. Maybe you could sit in front of a lighted candle or lie on your back on the floor with your arms and legs extended.

afternoon (1 ½ to 2 hours)

centering

Sing another song about God's hospitality. Or, sit
with your palms open in a spirit of receptivity.

meditation

A Story of Hospitality
in an Unexpected Place:

The Story of the Friendship
between Jesse Owens and Luz Long [17]

Leader: *Present this material in
a way that is comfortable for you.
One possibility is to read this
story aloud or ask a volunteer to
read it.*

This story, the telling of an unlikely friendship, is a tale of courage and compassion
and generosity. This story epitomizes the welcoming of the stranger in our midst. It is
a story of hospitality at its finest.

The year is 1936 at the summer Olympics in Berlin. Germany was the host. No
one would have dreamed back in 1931 when plans were made ahead, that five years
later Germany would be in the grip of the Third Reich and Adolph Hitler. Hitler
openly and unabashedly announced that the Olympic Games of 1936 would demon-
strate to the world once and for all the superiority of the Germans and the Aryan race
and the inferiority of the Jews and the Blacks whom he disdainfully labeled the "mon-
grel races." The highly charged Olympic Arena was filled with swastikas, and those in
power were proudly flying the fascist flag. In the opening procession, the United
States team was welcomed with whistles and jeers and vile insults, directed at its Jewish and Black teammates. The teams sympathetic to the Third Reich looked toward
Hitler's box and gave the Nazi salute. Into this terrifying and oppressive scenario of
propaganda and racism, entered the gifted athlete Jesse Owens, the son of an Alabama
cotton picker and the grandson of a slave. While still in high school, Owens won victo-
ries in national field and track events and set a record of 9.4 seconds in the 100-yard
dash—a record that lasted more than twenty years. While in college at Ohio State,
Owens tied the record for the 100-yard dash and set world records in the long jump,

the 220-yard low hurdles, and the 220-yard dash. His long-jump record, too, was not broken for another twenty-five years.

So when he went to Germany to compete in the 1936 Olympics, Jesse Owens was one of the finest athletes in the world. But even at the Olympics, Owens would first have to do well in the preliminary trials. And the trial in which he would have to prove himself the most was the broad jump. The broad jump was the event in which he was pitted against Hitler's acclaimed model of Aryan perfection, the perfectly built, blond-haired, blue-eyed Adonis named Luz Long. The competition, Owens knew, would be grueling. Not only was there the overwhelming psychological pressure of racism, there was a difference in climate. August in Berlin was muggier than Ann Arbor, Michigan, and Columbus, Ohio, where he had trained. The ground on the runway to the broad jump pit wasn't the same consistency he was used to. Just as the already nervous Jesse Owens was warming up for the preliminary in the broad jump, a newspaper reporter came over to him and asked, "Is it true Jesse? That Hitler walked out on you? That he wouldn't watch you jump?" It was true. Hitler had vacated the commandant's section of honor, refusing to watch a black athlete compete. It was at that moment that Jesse Owens' turn was called. Owens writes in his autobiography:

> I felt the energy surging into my legs and tingling in the muscles of my stomach as it never had before. I began my run, first almost in slow motion, then picking up speed, and finally faster and faster until I was moving almost as fast as I did during the 100 yd. dash. Suddenly the takeoff board was in front of me. I hit it, went up, up high—so high I knew I was outdoing [Luz] Long and every man who ever jumped.
>
> But they didn't measure it. I heard the referee shout "Foul!" in my ears before I ever came down. . . . I'd gone half a foot over the takeoff board.[18]

Destroyed psychologically by the bad jump, Owens tried a second broad jump and failed at that, too. Owens had one jump left to qualify for the Olympics and at the rate he was going, he felt doomed to fail. Owens writes:

> I looked around nervously, panic creeping into every cell of my body. On my right was Hitler's box. Empty. His way of saying I was a member of an inferior race and would give an inferior performance. In back of that box was a stadium

containing more than a hundred thousand people, almost all Germans, all wanting to see me fail.[19]

The pressure for Owens seemed unbearable; he began to panic; his legs began to shake; his teeth began to chatter. He was literally coming apart at the seams. Then, by some miracle, Jesse Owens discovered a hidden resource in the most unlikely place possible. He felt a hand on his arm, and he turned and looked into the sky-blue eyes of his archrival, the Aryan Enemy, Luz Long himself. The German athlete, his chief competitor, looked at him compassionately and said in broken English: "Look, there's no time to waste . . . [What's happened? Is it Hitler's pressure that has done this to you?] . . . you must jump . . . you must qualify." In those few seconds before Jesse Owens was called up to jump for the third and last time, the acclaimed German athlete Luz Long instructed Owens how not to jump the gun, how not to foul. He said: "You remeasure your steps. You take off six inches behind the foul board. You jump as hard as you can. [You'll be fine.]"

The German's unexpected kindness and insight emptied Owens of all of his panic like a syringe. His broad jump was a triumph! He succeeded where he had failed only moments before and qualified by more than a foot!

Most importantly, Jesse Owens and Luz Long began a friendship that lasted after the 1936 Olympics were over. At the Games themselves, whenever they weren't competing, they were talking together, learning about the other's life that was so different from their own. Luz Long talked to Jesse Owens about his ambivalence and confusion at where Germany was going under Hitler. Jesse Owens talked to Luz Long about his own difficulty in living in the United States where prejudice and racism still ran rampant. They would often end up chatting late into the night, much later than two fine Olympic champions should have had the good sense to do. Jesse Owens took home four gold medals in the 1936 Olympics: the 100-meter dash, the 200-meter dash, the 400-meter relay, and the broad jump itself, beating out his German friend. Owens writes:

> After [Luz] failed in his last attempt to beat me, he leaped out of the pit and raced to my side. To congratulate me. Then he walked toward the stands pulling me with him while Hitler was glaring, held up my hand and shouted to the gigantic crowd, "Jesse Owens! Jesse Owens!"[20]

Jesse Owens and Luz Long both resumed their everyday living after the Olympics but were able to keep up a faithful correspondence for three years until 1939. At that time, the war was in full swing. Finally no more letters arrived for Jesse Owens from his German friend. Luz Long died in the line of fire in the German army and was buried somewhere in the African desert.

Jesse Owens writes in his autobiography:

> Luz Long had been my competition in the Olympics. He was a white man—a Nazi white man who fought to destroy my country. I loved Luz Long, as much as my own brothers. I still love Luz Long. I went back to Berlin a few years ago and met his son, another fine young man. And I told Karl about his father. I told him that, though fate may have thrown us against one another, Luz rose above it, rose so high that I was left with not only four gold medals I would never had had, but with the priceless knowledge that the only human bond worth anything between human beings is their humanness.[21]

Luz Long and Jesse Owens broke down the barriers between them and extended hospitality to one another. It was only then that they could see how alike they really were.

---

journaling response
(allow about 15 minutes)

1. What is your first impression of this story?

2. This story clearly illustrates barriers to hospitality, which, in this friendship between Jesse Owens and Luz Long were overcome. What are some barriers to hospitality in our society today?

3. How can you yourself begin to overcome these barriers?

Leader: *Write these questions on newsprint and, instead of journaling, discuss with the whole group.*

interlude

Sing a song or take a stretch break before moving into the reflection time.

afternoon reflection
(allow about an hour)

Begin by playing a calming piece of music. Then gather your journal and art materials, and settle into a comfortable place where you can reflect on these questions and record your thoughts and feelings.

1. Hospitality To God

   • How are you making room for God?
   • How are you welcoming your relationship with God?
   • How are you nurturing your prayer life?

2. Hospitality To Self

   • How are you taking care of yourself?
   • How are you providing encouragement for yourself to grow?
   • How are you forgiving yourself and treating yourself gently?

3. Hospitality To Others

   • How are you being hospitable to others:
       in your family?
       in your workplace?
       in your church or faith community?
       in your town?
       across the world?
   • Whom are you excluding from "the welcome table"?

Leader: *Have the reflection questions written on newsprint ahead of time so people can copy them into their journals (or have them printed on handouts). Direct people to take their journals and some art materials to a place where they can quietly respond to the questions. Let them know they will have 30 minutes. Then gather everyone back together by singing a song, if you wish. Divide people into groups of 4, counting off by the letters R-O-O-M, if the numbers come out right. Invite them to discuss each area of hospitality for 10 minutes, sharing what is comfortable from their journaling. Let them know you will keep time and signal them (perhaps with a bell or some other nonintrusive sound) when it is time to move on to the next topic.*

4. Using your art materials, draw an image of whom you are excluding from "the welcome table." Remember, the goal is not to create a work of art but to let an alternative form of expression give you some new insight.

- What emotions are you experiencing as you create this image?
- Meditate on your image and use it as a catalyst for prayer.
- How might you bring about change?

CLOSING RITUAL

BLESSING: A blessing is always a sign of hospitality, affirmation, and encouragement. Write a blessing for yourself. Add a gesture or touch to accompany the words. Now bless yourself.

SONG: If you wish, sing "Blessed Be the Tie That Binds" or another hymn of God's hospitality.

Leader: *Ask the participants to stand and gather in a circle, pairing off. (If there is an odd number, one group of three can stand together.) Ask them to bless the other person or persons with the blessing of words and gesture they wrote for themselves.*

- SUGGESTION ONE

Hospitality To God and To Yourself

Consider using some or all of the "Practicing Sabbath" retreat on page 11. Sabbath is about hospitality to God as well as to oneself.

- SUGGESTION TWO

Bible Study

Check out Micah and hospitality. Study Micah 6:1-8. This is a potent passage worthy of prayer and focus.

Leader: *Ask participants to study Micah 6:1-8 in solitude. Then ask them to divide into small groups of 3-5 to talk together about God's hospitality to God's people and the people's hospitality (or lack thereof) to God.*

- SUGGESTION THREE

A Recipe for Hospitality

Write a recipe for hospitality on an index or recipe card. Start with a list of ingredients and then write about preparation. Don't forget to mention how many people the "dish" will serve and what else goes with it.[22]

Leader: *Hand out recipe cards to each participant. After giving people time to write their recipe for hospitality, invite anyone who wishes to share what they have written. You may want to bring along a recipe box and ask who's willing to put theirs into the box for others to read for the duration of the retreat.*

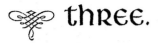 **three.**

practicing prayer and action:

living a life of intercession

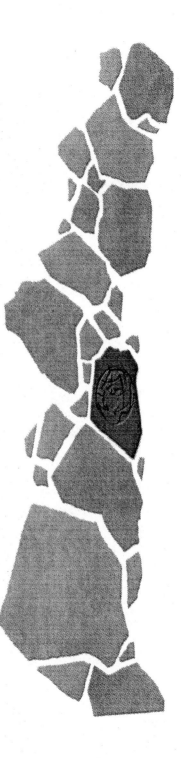

Let us together live a life of intercession.
—letter to Rev. Ed Beers from Brother Christopher, monk of Taizé

. . . prayer is more a way of being than an isolated act of doing. [23]
—Tilden Edwards, *Living in the Presence*

theme

This retreat is an invitation to examine a life of intercessory prayer and the subsequent fruits of action and social justice, and to explore what it means to live "a life of intercession."

planning ahead

One week before your day of retreat, ponder the following questions for reflection and let them simmer as you go about your daily activities:

How would you define "a life of intercession"?
What would be your requirements for living such a life?
How are prayer and action connected in your life?

Before your retreat day, collect the following materials, so you won't be distracted during your retreat:

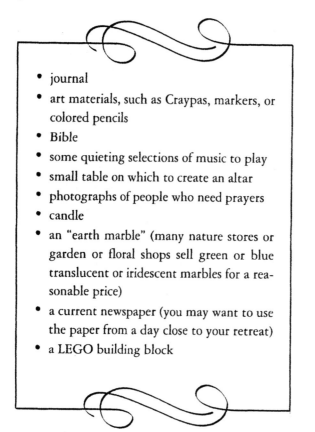

- journal
- art materials, such as Craypas, markers, or colored pencils
- Bible
- some quieting selections of music to play
- small table on which to create an altar
- photographs of people who need prayers
- candle
- an "earth marble" (many nature stores or garden or floral shops sell green or blue translucent or iridescent marbles for a reasonable price)
- a current newspaper (you may want to use the paper from a day close to your retreat)
- a LEGO building block

If you are doing this retreat with a group . . .

Leader: *Reflect on these questions for your own preparation. Pray for yourself and each retreat participant.*

Leader: *In addition to asking people bring a journal and a Bible, you will need to supply some art materials. Also, an easel with newsprint and markers is helpful. You will need to get an "earth marble" and a LEGO for each participant, and have several current newspapers available. Practice reading the guided imagery on pages 48-49 so that you are comfortable with leading it during the retreat.*

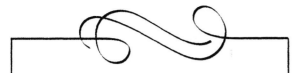

- Look over the guided imagery prayer on pages 48-49 and decide whether you want to make, in advance, a tape of yourself reading it aloud or whether you want to read it and pray it when the time comes.

- *Optional:* music for "We Shall Overcome" or another song of prayer and action; music for "He's Got the Whole World in His Hands" or another song of prayer, justice, or peace; music for "This Is My Song"[1] (to the tune of "Finlandia"); recording of "Silent Night/7 O'clock News" by Simon and Garfunkle (available on "Parsley, Sage, Rosemary and Thyme," a part of "Collected Works," a 3-disk set on the Columbia label, or on "Old Friends," a 3-disk set on Legacy Records). If this recording is not available, choose another recording that challenges social apathy or a song that connects prayer and action.

CREATING SACRED SPACE

Create an altar by arranging on a small table the photographs you have collected of people who need prayers. Place a lighted candle in the middle.

MORNING [2 to 2 ½ hours]

welcome

Welcome this new day. Stretch your arms toward the sky, inhaling deeply your hopes for this day, exhaling whatever anxieties you wish to put aside. After repeating this several times, consider singing or playing a favorite piece of music to quiet your heart.

Leader: After leading the group in some stretching and breathing, your welcome should include a description of the day's theme. Suggest a song for the group to sing together or play a quieting piece of music.

centering

Sit for a few minutes in silence with your hands open on your lap, receptive to God's leading. Breathe in connection. Breathe out separation. Repeat this several times. Prayerfully ponder and review the distractions or obstacles that may be blocking you from receiving this retreat fully. Pass these over to God's loving care. Sit for a few minutes in silence and offer a prayer of invocation asking God's blessing on your retreat.

Leader: After this time of centering and prayer, allow some time for introductions. If the group is less than twenty, go around the circle sharing the following: "Name a time when your life was changed by praying for someone else or by being prayed for." If the group is larger, have people share in smaller groups. (See Appendix B for other Welcoming Suggestions.)

scripture

Read Romans 8:26-27.

meditation

A Life of Intercession

Leader: Present this material in a way that is comfortable for you. Adapt this meditation any way you like, or create your own.

On May 7, 1997 I attended a retreat I will never forget. It was called "A Life of Intercession" and was led by my friend and colleague Ed Beers of Madison, Wisconsin. At the end of that rich day, my head and heart were full to bursting. I drove back home pondering the phrase "a life of intercession" over and over again. What would living that kind of life require?

The word "intercessory," as in "intercessory prayer," and the word "intercession" are based on the Latin verb *intercedere*, which means "to be situated between" or "to be present among." Perhaps we could say then that a life of intercession is a life situated between divinity and humanity, a life made present among the joys and sufferings of others.

I have been pondering the meaning of a "life of intercession" for some time now, and have come to recognize that there are at least three requirements for a life of intercession.

The first requirement of a life of intercession is offering to another the gift of taking time to pray.

Six years ago, long before I attended his retreat, Ed Beers called me from Madison. He said, "Holly, I'm making calls about my list of intercessions, and I've been praying for your brother-in-law Bart. How is he doing?" Although Bart had recently died of colon cancer at age 42, I realized that Ed Beers had been praying continuously for Bart for a year. Ed inspires me profoundly because he spends at least an hour each day praying on behalf of others. He feels strongly that intercessory prayer is not to be entered into half-heartedly or in a rushed manner, but slowly and fully. He offers this practice of prayer the time it deserves. I never flippantly ask Ed to pray for someone because I know he will devote himself totally to that task.

The second requirement of a life of intercession is trusting in God.

For most of us, this is not an easy step. Do any of us fully comprehend the releasing power of the words "thy will be done," which we pray in the Lord's prayer each Sunday? Thy will be done: that means trusting implicitly that God is working alongside us for good, trusting that God's judgment is wiser and deeper than our own. By trusting God, we align our own will with God's will. The beloved scripture from Romans 8:26 reminds us that "we do not know how to pray as we ought, but . . . [the] Spirit intercedes [for us] with sighs too deep for words."

I have learned a great deal about trust in God from my Quaker friends, who when asked to pray, will say simply, "I will hold you in the Light." This prayer of absolute trust, this prayer which delights in God's awesome wisdom, sits in contrast to the highly controlled wish list of desired outcomes that many of us frequently present to God. This kind of prayer finds its peace in any outcome that God thinks best. It is a prayer of surrender to the larger picture of God's love.

The third requirement of a life of intercession is living a life of integrity and justice; in other words, walking the talk.

Not long ago, as I was running errands in my neighborhood, I was both amused and perplexed by a huge, late model, red-and-gold Cadillac with a vanity license plate that read "Psalm 92." When I arrived home, I decided I needed to brush up on that particular psalm and discovered that it says that the righteous will flourish. The driver of that flashy Cadillac must have felt very righteous indeed! I wonder if the owner of that handsome vehicle was righteous enough to volunteer at a soup kitchen or to help in an inner-city literacy program?

A life of intercession means living a life consistent with justice, a life that may entail entering into the sufferings of others. In Isaiah, Yahweh says to the Israelites, "Because there is blood on your hands, I will not listen to your prayer" (paraphrase of Isaiah 1:15). God does not respect those whose inner life and outer life are not consistent, whose prayer and action remain disconnected. In her book *Dance of the Spirit*, teacher and theologian Maria Harris suggests what she calls "a diet of spiritual nourishment." Included in her diet of spiritual nourishment are one weekly participation in a human rights group and one evening a week working for justice.[24] It is through this kind of practice that we come to understand others' needs and gifts as well as our own. When we build a house for Habitat for Humanity, we understand more clearly the needs of the urban poor. When we volunteer for Amnesty International, we begin to grasp what it's like to be a prisoner isolated from the rest of humanity. When we collect pledges and participate in a CROP (Christian Rural Overseas Program) walk, we know what it feels like to pound the pavement in solidarity with the hungry of the world. During the civil rights movement, activist William Sloane Coffin asked Rabbi Abraham Joshua Heschel, "Why do you march?" Rabbi Heschel responded, "In order to pray."

I have often said that my favorite part of the worship service at my church is what we call "Joys and Concerns." I am often weeping my way through Joys and Concerns, but it is, nevertheless, the best part. Joys and Concerns is one small way in which I practice living a life of intercession each week. For it is in that time of raising our hands and speaking, and in that time of praying for and with one another, that we learn of our most heartfelt celebrations and fears and struggles. It is in that time of intercession that we commit ourselves to prayer and possibly action as well.

Prayer changes the one who prays. If we pray for a person, it is much more likely that we will visit that person in the hospital or take that person a meal. Douglas Steere says "whether we intend it or not, to pray for another is to become involved in his or her life. For one who wants to avoid being drawn into costly involvement, intercessory prayer is to be shunned like the plague."[25] Through our intercessions for one another, our horizons are expanded and our worldview changed. It is at that point that our prayer leads us into action.

Think again about the Latin verb *intercedere* and what it means to be "situated between" or to be "present among." Living a life of intercession means taking time to pray, trusting in God, and walking the talk. It means living a life connected to God and connected with others.

MORNING REFLECTION [allow about an hour]

Play a quieting piece of music. Then gather your journal and some art materials, and settle into a comfortable place where you can reflect on these questions and record your thoughts and feelings.

1. Many people would agree that prayer changes the one who prays. What is your experience of this?

2. The first requirement of a life of intercession is offering to another the gift of taking time to pray.
   - How and when and where do you pray for other people?
   - Are you satisfied with your practice of prayer?
   - Is there anything you would like to change?

Leader: *Have the journaling questions written on newsprint ahead of time so people can copy them into their journals (or have them printed on handouts). Direct people to take their journals and some art materials to a place where they can quietly respond to the questions. Let them know they will have 30 minutes. Then gather everyone back together by singing a song, if you wish. Divide people into groups of 4, counting off by P-R-A-Y, if the numbers come out right. Invite them to discuss each requirement for 10 minutes, sharing what is comfortable from their journaling and drawing. Let them know you will keep time and signal them (perhaps with a chime or bell or some other nonintrusive sound) when it is time to move on to the next topic.*

3. The second requirement of a life of intercession is trusting in God.

- Whom do you know who demonstrates his or her faith through a profound trust in God?
- How have you come to know this?

4. The third requirement of a life of intercession is walking the talk, living a life of integrity and justice. Teresa of Avila, a sixteenth century mystic wrote this:

> *Christ has no body now on earth but yours;*
> *yours are the only hands*
> *with which he can do his work,*
> *yours are the only feet*
> *with which he can go about the world,*
> *yours are the only eyes*
> *through which his compassion*
> *can shine forth upon a troubled world.*
> *Christ has no body on earth now but yours.*[26]

Using your art materials, create an image that represents these passionate words of St. Teresa. Let your hand go where it will, without trying to direct it from your head, and see what happens. When you have finished, consider how you are walking the talk. What more would you like to do?

SONG

Sing "We Shall Overcome," or another song of prayer and action.

a prayer before eating

Gracious God, Source of Life, I pray for my hungry brothers and sisters across the world. I pray that they may be fed and that the reasons they are hungry may be confronted. I pray in gratitude, O Holy One, for my food and for all the people and places that have brought it to my table. Thanks be to you, O God. Amen.

Leader: *Lead this prayer aloud, changing the "I" to "we." Stand and hold hands in a circle.*

lunch and free time [2 hours]

Optional question to ponder during free time:

*How am I connecting
prayer and action
in my life?*

If possible, walk outside, absorb the season, notice nature. If you can't go outside, consider relaxing with a new symbol or a new posture. Maybe you could sit in front of a lighted candle or lie on your back on the floor with your arms and legs extended.

afternoon [1 ½ to 2 hours]

centering

Sing "He's Got the Whole World in His Hands" or another song of prayer, justice, or peace. You may want to alternate verses and pronouns: "She's Got the Whole World in Her Hands." Or, sit with your palms open in a spirit of receptivity.

meditation

Holding the World in God's Light: A Guided Imagery Prayer [27]

When you see the earth from the moon,
you don't see any divisions there of nations or states.
This might be the symbol, really,
for the new mythology to come.
That is the country
that we are going to be celebrating.
And those are the people that we are one with. [28]

Leader: *Pass out "earth marbles." Invite anyone who wishes to share aloud any situations or groups of people around the world for whom they wish the group to pray. Then read the guided imagery very slowly, with plenty of pauses, while participants sit comfortably with their eyes closed. At the end, encourage people to take their earth marbles home and put them in a place where they will be reminded of the need for intercessory prayer.*

At the beginning of this time of reflection, hold your "earth marble" in your hand. Letting the marble represent our planet, think about any international news you have heard recently. Name in your heart any situations or groups of people around the world for whom you wish to pray.

Read the following guided imagery prayer very slowly (or play your tape, if you have recorded this imagery in advance). Provide ample time for reflection between phrases.

You are going to be spending a few minutes in a prayer of guided meditation. Get comfortable. Take anything heavy off your lap. Close your eyes. Take a couple of slow, deep breaths . . . in and out. Feel yourself holding the planet in your hand.

Imagine the earth surrounded by the Healing Light of God . . . See our planet radiant and glowing in God's Light . . .

As you think about the whole earth, picture in your mind your own community. Where are the divisions? Where is the fear? Where is the tension? . . . Imagine your own community bathed in God's love.

Again, picture the globe. Move in your mind to the east. Move to a part of the world east of you that particularly needs healing. Imagine those people held in God's Light. Picture the people there comforted and at peace. [28]

Taking all the time you need, continue moving slowly around the world, stopping from place to place. Remain with whatever people need help and hold them in the Light of God. Travel in your mind around the world . . . (Pause for at least two minutes.)

Imagine your hands and feet becoming the hands and feet of God. Picture yourself carrying the Spirit of God out into your community and throughout the world. How might this happen?

When you are ready, open your eyes and come back to this place and this room.

Save your earth marble and keep it in a place where you are likely to come across it each day. In this way, you will be reminded of the need for intercessory prayer and advocacy for sisters and brothers around the world.

SONG

Play a recording of "Silent Night/7 O'clock News," if you have been able to find it. If this is not available, choose another recording that challenges social apathy or sing a song that connects prayer and action.

afternoon Reflection

(allow about an hour)

1. Set a section of a current newspaper in front of you. Look at the headlines and pray for people in need of prayer.

2. Set a LEGO building block in front of you. Pray with a "LEGO" focus.[29]

   - L stands for loved ones. Pray for them.
   - E stands for enemies. Consider your "enemies." Pray for them.*
   - G stands for those in need of guidance and grace. Pray for them.
   - O stands for ourselves. Spend some time praying for yourself.

Leader: *Hand out a number of sections of both local and national current newspapers that contain headlines of people in need of prayer. Give a LEGO building block to each person. After the time of solitude and prayer, discuss as a group.*

* A note on praying for your enemies: Author Jane Redmont tells the story of a mother whose twenty-seven-year-old son was a soldier in the Gulf War. She wanted to pray for the safety of her child, but she also knew the depth of concern of all the mothers on both sides of the conflict. She found a way to pray that was inclusive. As she prayed for her son, she would image an anonymous Iraqi mother praying for her child who was a soldier on the other side.[30] Consider: Who are your enemies? Close your fists tightly and release them. Do this several times. Put yourself in your enemy's shoes. Continue praying.

closing ritual

PRAYER: Name in your heart anything for which you are joyous and thankful and any concerns for which prayer is needed. Sit in silence for about five minutes praying in intercession.

SONG: Sing "This Is My Song" (to the tune of "Finlandia") or read it aloud, if you wish.

This is my song, O God of all the nations,
a song of peace for lands afar and mine.
This is my home, the country where my heart is;
here are my hopes, my dreams, my holy shrine;
But other hearts in other lands are beating
with hopes and dreams as true and high as mine.

My country's skies are bluer than the ocean,
and sunlight beams on cloverleaf and pine;
But other lands have sunlight, too, and clover,
and skies are everywhere as blue as mine.
O hear my song, O God of all the nations,
a song of peace for their land and for mine.[31]

COMMISSION: Read aloud this commission by John Wesley:

Do all the good you can
By all the means you can
In all the ways you can
In all the places you can
To all the people you can
As long as ever you can.[32]
Amen!

Leader: *Invite participants to randomly share aloud. After participants' joys and concerns are spoken, all sit in silence for about five minutes, praying in intercession.*

Leader: *Write on newsprint and read in unison or have the participants repeat each line back to you.*

• SUGGESTION ONE

Bible Study

Check out the Great Judgment. Study Matthew 25:31-46. This is a powerful passage deserving of prayer. Take time to pray for the groups of people mentioned in this scripture. In your journal, consider the following questions:

How might your prayer lead you into action?
How may God be calling you to respond to this scripture?

Leader: *After participants have had some time for Bible study in solitude, invite them to come back together. Then write the two questions on newsprint. Discuss.*

• SUGGESTION TWO

The Magnificat Prayer

Study and pray with the Magnificat, the Canticle or Song of Mary, Luke 1:46-55. (You may want to place the Magnificat in context and read all of Luke 1:5-56.) Here is one delightfully worded version:

I acclaim the greatness of the Lord,
I delight in God my savior,
who regarded my humble state.
Truly from this day on
all ages will call me blest.

For God, wonderful in power,
has used that strength for me.
Holy the name of the Lord!
whose mercy embraces the faithful,
one generation to the next.

The mighty arm of God
scatters the proud in their conceit,
pulls tyrants from their thrones,
and raises up the humble.
The Lord fills the starving
and lets the rich go hungry.

God rescues lowly Israel,
recalling the promise of mercy,
the promise made to our ancestors,
to Abraham's heirs for ever.[33]

Write a haiku about Mary or about what you hear in the Magnificat. Haiku is a popular form of Japanese poetry, containing seventeen syllables: five in the first line, seven in the second line, and five in the third line. Here is an example:

a trusting Mary
overshadowed by Spirit
bore a divine child

• SUGGESTION THREE (for groups)

Prayer Partners

Leader: *Invite those who wish to share their poetry.*

Leader: *Encourage those who wish to pair up into prayer partners at the beginning of the retreat. Remind them that all prayer concerns are to be held in confidence unless partners agree otherwise. Then give them these instructions or write on newsprint: Talk about what prayers you would like your partner to be sharing with God on your behalf. Continue praying for your prayer partner throughout the retreat. Take time to talk a bit about the experience of praying for one another and decide if you want to keep in touch in any way after the retreat.*

 # four.

practicing the fast:

an invitation to relinquishment and self-emptying

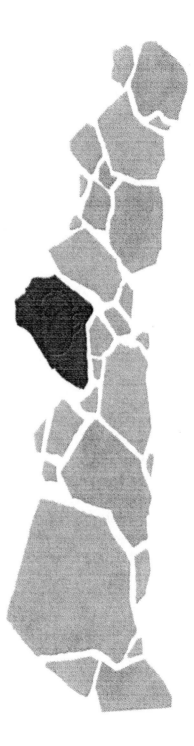

. . . I humbled my soul with fasting.
—Psalm 69:10

When what we consume is consuming us, and what we possess is possessing us, the only way back to health and balance is to refrain from using those things that have control over us.[34]
—Marjorie J. Thompson, *Soul Feast*

theme

This retreat explores fasting as a summons to surrender and self-emptying and is an invitation to take a look at things to which you might be overly attached.

planning ahead

One week before your day of retreat, ponder the following questions for reflection and let them simmer as you go about your daily activities:

What does fasting mean to you?

Have you ever fasted from something—whether food or activity or a specific comfort? If so, what did that experience teach you?

How might God be asking you to empty yourself?

Before your retreat day, collect the following materials, so you won't be distracted during your retreat:

- journal
- art materials, such as Craypas, markers, or colored pencils
- Bible
- some quieting selections of music to play
- small table on which to create an altar
- a plain sheet of paper (for the altar)
- a cup (or two cups, if you want one on your altar and one for meditation)
- a candle
- *Optional:* music for "Be Thou My Vision"; music for "Jesus Calls Us, O'er the Tumult" or another song of surrender

If you are doing this retreat with a group . . .

Leader: *Reflect on these questions for your own preparation. Pray for yourself and each retreat participant.*

Leader: *Ask everyone to bring a journal, a Bible, and an empty cup. In addition, you will need to supply some art materials. Also, an easel with newsprint and markers is helpful.*

CREATING SACRED SPACE

Write in large letters on a piece of paper the following question:

> *"How can I empty myself*
> *so that I may receive God?"*

Create an altar by placing your sign on a table next to the empty cup you have selected. (Let it lie flat or prop it up.) Add a lighted candle.

MORNING (2 to 2 ½ hours)

WELCOME

Welcome this new day. Stretch your arms toward the sky, inhaling deeply your hopes for this day, exhaling whatever anxieties you wish to put aside. After repeating this several times, consider singing or playing a favorite piece of music to quiet your heart.

Leader: *After leading the group in some stretching and breathing, your welcome should include a description of the day's theme. Suggest a song for the group to sing together or play a quieting piece of music.*

CENTERING

Sit for a few minutes in silence with our hands open on your lap, receptive to God's leading. Breathe in clarity. Breath out clutter. Repeat this several times. Prayerfully ponder and review the distractions or obstacles which may be blocking you from receiving this retreat fully. Pass these over to God's loving care. Sit for a few minutes in silence and offer a prayer of invocation asking God's blessing on your retreat.

Leader: *After this time of centering and prayer, allow some time for introductions. If the group is less than twenty, go around the circle answering the questions: "Have you ever fasted from something? What did you learn?" If the group is larger, have people share in smaller groups. (See Appendix B for other Welcoming Suggestions.)*

scripture

Read Matthew 4:1-4.

meditation

Reclaiming the Fast

Leader: *Present this material in a way that is comfortable for you. Adapt this meditation any way you like, or create your own.*

Not long ago I was chatting with a colleague who asked me if I could shed any light on the whole subject of Lent and fasting. First, I responded by saying that I was much more of a "feaster" than a "faster." Then I offered my opinion that fasting, as I understood it, was really a broad summons to abstinence: abstinence from anything to which we are addicted or overly attached. That could be alcohol or sex or food or TV or shopping or busyness, just about anything that we wildly crave and that has some likelihood of preventing us from being whom God created us to be. "Fasting," I commented to my friend, "may not imply just giving up food, but anything that makes us crazy, driven, or obsessed."

Historically, fasting from food (and perhaps water, too) has served as an invitation to humility and personal or national repentance. Fasting also has served as an invitation to inner preparedness for a difficult mission, as in the forty-day wilderness fasts of Moses (Deuteronomy 9:9) and Elijah (I Kings 19:8) and Jesus (Matthew 4:2). Fasting boasts an impressive biblical track record. Some of our best known biblical characters were faithful fasters: David the King, Esther the Queen, Daniel the Seer, Paul the Apostle.

Today, for many religious people, fasting is an invitation to clear-sightedness. When we fast or abstain from something with which we are overly familiar, our vision becomes less cloudy and more penetrating.

Once when I was a student in a class for artists, the teacher asked us to refrain from indulging in all forms of media for one week. We were not allowed to read books or magazines or newspapers; we were not permitted to listen to music or radio; we were not allowed to turn on the TV. I did not cope well with this assignment and sheepishly gave up after two days. I was bored to death. It was a sobering spiritual lesson; it had become painfully obvious that I craved constant stimulation.

Through fasting, we identify quickly those things to which we are overly attached, those forces that control us. When we fast, we can easily see how addicted we have become to the nonessentials, and how that attachment has gotten in the way of a deeper relationship with God. When we fast, we suddenly realize the shallowness of our dependencies and addictions, and how far removed our spiritual selves have migrated from what really counts. When we fast from food, we come to understand how much we rely on certain edible favorites to placate our anger or soothe our anxiety. When we fast from buying new things, we see how possessing that new item was an attempt to fill another deeper emptiness. When we abstain from anything, we see clearly what we have been substituting for a friendship with God.

If you feel a need to get your life back in balance, consider fasting. It can help what is murky become clear.

MORNING REFLECTION [allow about an hour]

Sing a song, such as "Be Thou My Vision," or play a quieting piece of music. Then gather your journal and settle into a comfortable place where you can reflect on these questions and record your thoughts and feelings in your journal.

1. What do you do to excess?[35] What might be distracting you from God?

2. Fasting is often associated with letting go. To what are you feeling overly attached? Is there something in your life that it might be time to let go of?

3. Fasting can mean giving up harmful ways of behaving, such as driving yourself relentlessly and expecting others to do the same. What kind of behaviors do you indulge in that separate you from God or other people? What harmful ways of behaving would you like to give up? Sit for a while and pray about this.

Leader: *Have the journaling questions written on newsprint ahead of time so people can copy them into their journals (or have them printed on handouts). Direct people to take their journals to a place where they can quietly respond to the questions. Let them know they will have 40 minutes. Then gather everyone back together by singing a song, if you wish. Divide people into groups of 4, counting off by F-A-S-T, if the numbers come out right. Invite them to share for 20 minutes what is comfortable from their journaling and drawing.*

Interlude

Sit quietly for a moment and meditate on the word "relinquishment."

Leader: *Choose a song to sing together before lunch, if you wish.*

A Prayer Before Eating

Gracious God, Source of Life, until I understand fasting, I cannot fully comprehend feasting. Thank you for all my sources of abundance. Thank you for your generosity and hospitality. Thank you for my food. Amen.

Leader: *Lead this prayer aloud, changing the "I" to "we," and "my" to "our." Stand and hold hands in a circle.*

Lunch and Free Time (2 hours)

Optional question to ponder during free time:

*How can I empty myself
so that there is more room for God?*

If possible, walk outside, absorb the season, notice nature. If you can't go outside, consider relaxing with a new symbol or a new posture. Maybe you could sit in front of a lighted candle or lie on your back on the floor with your arms and legs extended.

Afternoon (1½ to 2 hours)

Centering

Play or sing a song about the spiritual life. Or, sit with your palms open in a spirit of receptivity.

meditation

Some Thoughts on Fasting

Leader: *Write each of these quotations and questions on separate sheets of newsprint ahead of time, or print them on handouts. (If the quotations are displayed on newsprint, allow time for participants to copy them). Read each quotation and question aloud, section by section, and give the group 10 minutes for discussion—either as a whole group or in smaller groups—before moving onto the next quotation.*

Read each of the following quotations and use the journaling questions to guide your reflection time.

❦ THOUGHT ❦

"[Fasting] draws us toward simplicity . . . the relinquishment of immediate impulses to eat can have a way of reducing the grasping in my mind for all kinds of things. . . . A certain sufficiency and ease of the moment emerges. There is room for God to rise lightly in consciousness and for the heaviness of ego to subside."[36]—Tilden Edwards, *Living in the Presence*

How have you experienced simplicity as making room for God?

❦ THOUGHT ❦

"The discipline of fasting has to do with the critical dynamic of accepting those limits which are life-restoring."[37]—Marjorie Thompson, *Soul Feast*

How do you understand limits that are life-restoring?

"I glanced around Morrie's study. It was the same today as it had been the first day I arrived. The books held their same places on the shelves. The papers cluttered the same old desk. The outside rooms had not been improved or upgraded. In fact, Morrie really hadn't bought anything new—except medical equipment—in a long, long time, maybe years. The day he learned that he was terminally ill was the day he lost interest in his purchasing power."[38]—Mitch Albom, *Tuesdays with Morrie*

How does the clarity induced by illness compare to the clarity induced by a fast?
Can you speak from personal experience?
What lessons might be learned from both?

interlude

Sing a song or take a stretch break before moving into the reflection time.

afternoon reflection
[allow about an hour]

Gather your journal and some art materials, and settle into a comfortable place where you can reflect on these questions. Set a cup before you and play a quieting selection of music as you contemplate its emptiness. Consider the following questions, using your journal to record your thoughts and feelings.

Let us remain as empty as possible
so that God can fill us up.[39]
—Mother Teresa

Leader: *Have the journaling questions written on newsprint ahead of time so people can copy them into their journals (or have them printed on handouts). Direct people to take their journals, some art materials, and the cup they brought to a place where they can quietly respond to the questions. Let them know they will have 40 minutes. Then gather everyone back together by singing a song, if you wish. Divide people into groups of 5, counting off by the letters E-M-P-T-Y, if the numbers come out right. Invite them to share for 20 minutes what is comfortable from their journaling and drawing.*

1. Sometimes emptiness is confused with boredom. What do you do when you're bored? What causes you to be anxious? What favorite anxiety-relieving habits do you resort to when you're bored? Make a list. Examine it prayerfully. How does boredom differ from a true spiritual emptying? How might God help?

2. What gifts may God be trying to offer you that you are too full to receive? Using your art materials, draw the outline of a large cup. In images or words, fill in the cup with those things that are making your life too full or that are blocking your availability to God. What is your picture showing you?

3. Ask yourself again, "What gifts may God be trying to offer me that I am are too full to receive?" Place your hands on top of one another to represent fullness. Don't rush. Sit for a while . . .

Sit and pray as you contemplate the empty cup you have set before you. Cup your hands together. How is God calling you to empty yourself?

closing Ritual

CONFESSION: Place your empty cup on the floor about a foot in front of you. Say this sentence out loud, finishing with whatever comes to mind.

"I confess that I am too full of _____."

Leader: *Ask everyone to sit or stand in a circle, holding hands, with their cups in front of them. People may confess aloud if they wish, or silently in their hearts. You may want to offer your own words aloud first in order to get things going.*

PRAYER: Forgive my excesses, O God. Empty me of my addictions and those things which control me. Help me to make room for your gifts. Fill me with yourself. Amen.

SONG: Consider singing "Jesus Calls Us, O'er the Tumult" or another song of surrender.

Leader: *Pray the closing prayer changing the language from "my" to "our" and "me" to "us."*

৵৵ to plan a longer retreat

Making Room for God

Create a new retreat called "Making Room for God" by combining the "Practicing Sabbath" retreat on page 11 and this "Practicing the Fast" retreat together into one longer weekend retreat. The theme of the new retreat could be described in the following way.

THEME: This retreat challenges us to think about how we go about making room for God in our busy lives. It focuses on inviting God to act in our lives through (1) our observance of Sabbath, and (2) our practice of relinquishment: taking a good look at those things that we do to excess and that keep God at a distance.

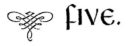 **five.**

practicing
giving back to god

on loan to love

The earth is the LORD'S
and all that is in it,
the world,
and those who live in it.
—Psalm 24:1

theme

This stewardship retreat examines the preciousness of our relationships and our shared struggle in letting go. Just as we do not own the earth, we do not own anything God has created, including our loved ones.

planning ahead

One week before your day of retreat, ponder the following questions for reflection and let them simmer as you go about your daily activities:

*What is your understanding of stewardship
or giving back to God?
How do you practice stewardship?*

Before your retreat day, collect the following materials, so you won't be distracted during your retreat:

- journal
- art materials, such as Craypas, markers, or colored pencils
- Bible
- some quieting selections of music to play (nature recordings that incorporate running water, singing of birds, chirping of insects, etc. may be useful in creating your retreat environment)
- small table on which to create an altar
- materials for your altar table: collect some things of beauty that God has created, perhaps a leaf, a shell, a rock, a plant. You may want to include pictures of individual people or animals. A candle with leaves or pine cones embedded in the wax would be especially appropriate to light on this retreat.
- some Play-Doh or some clay
- a photo of a loved one

If you are doing this retreat with a group . . .

Leader: *Reflect on these questions for your own preparation. Pray for yourself and each retreat participant.*

Leader: *Ask each person to bring a photo of a loved one, along with a journal and a Bible. In addition, you will need to supply some art materials and an easel with newsprint and markers. You will also need to bring enough Play-Doh or clay for each person. Play-Doh comes in little party-favor 1-oz. cans that can be found at drugstores, party stores, or toy stores in the party favor section. Or, use other clay, possibly the air-dry clay available at art stores. If you choose the jewelry-making option for the longer retreat, you will need enough supplies for your group.*

- *Optional:* music for "For the Beauty of the Earth," "Morning has Broken," and "All Things Bright and Beautiful"
- *For longer retreats:* a globe of the earth (any size). If you choose the jewelry-making option, you will need some jewelry-making supplies, such as sheets of cardboard or posterboard in various colors, scraps of decorative paper and fabric, greeting cards, assorted small beads, ribbon, yarn, embroidery floss, nature stickers. Pinbacks may be purchased in small bags or in bulk at any craft store and can be attached using any household cement. You should also have some glue and a pair of scissors.

CREATING SACRED SPACE

Create an altar table by arranging the things of God's beauty you have collected.

MORNING (2 to 2 ½ hours)

welcome

Welcome this new day. Stretch your arms toward the sky, inhaling deeply your hopes for this day, exhaling whatever anxieties you wish to put aside. After repeating this several times, consider singing or playing a favorite piece of music to quiet your heart. If you like it, "For the Beauty of the Earth" would work well.

Leader: *After leading the group in some stretching and breathing, your welcome should include a description of the day's theme. Suggest a song for the group to sing together or play a quieting piece of music. "For the Beauty of the Earth" is a good one.*

CENTERING

Sit for a few minutes in silence with your hands open on your lap, receptive to God's leading. Breathe in abundance. Breathe out scarcity. Repeat this several times. Prayerfully ponder and review the distractions or obstacles which may be blocking you from receiving this retreat fully. Pass these over to God's loving care. Sit for a few minutes in silence and offer a prayer of invocation asking God's blessing on your retreat.

Leader: After this time of centering and prayer, allow some time for introductions. If the group is less than twenty, go around the circle sharing the following: "What photo did you bring? Tell us briefly why you brought that particular one." If the group is larger, have people share in smaller groups. (See Appendix B for other Welcoming Suggestions).

SCRIPTURE

Read Psalm 100 and John 1:1-5.

MEDITATION

On Loan to Love

Leader: Present this material in a way that is comfortable for you. Adapt this meditation any way you like, or create your own.

When you think of the word "stewardship," the first thing that comes to mind is probably money. But there is another very important aspect of stewardship to consider today: the stewardship of people. Whenever members of a church celebrate an infant baptism or dedication, they are recognizing that child as a child of God's and agreeing, as stewards, to care for that child of God.

For all of us who are parents, it is tempting to believe that it is we who have created our children. When our children look adorable or act precocious or perform clever tricks, we're tempted to murmur proudly, "Just think, I created that child. I must be pretty terrific to produce a kid like that." But then we pause and sheepishly remember, with awe and wonder, the miracle of that child's creation. When we step back and think, we realize that we actually had very little to do with that marvelous act. When we're honest, we resonate with the psalmist who writes: "Know ye that the LORD is God: it is [God] that hath made us, and not we ourselves" (*KJV*).

In most stewardship sermons, there is one dominant theme: God has given us everything we have, and so we are held responsible for taking care of it. Without God we would have nothing. Think about how this applies to the stewardship of people. God has given us everything, including all other persons, particularly our children. Just as we do not *own* the land, or the mountains, or the seas, we do not *own* our children. They are ours to borrow for a lifetime, to protect, to educate, to nurture, to care for. They are on loan to love.

In our eagerness, however, to take care of our children, we sometimes forget that we are their caretakers merely until they are old enough to strike out on their own. They belong to God and not to us. We forget that part of the stewardship of loving is in the letting go.

In the last several months, I got a touching calligraphied card from a dear friend who knew I was struggling with letting my children grow up. The card's message read: "There are only two lasting bequests we can hope to give our children. One of these is roots, the other wings." But that gift of wings, that setting free, is never easy, whether it comes as the infant goes off to the babysitter's, the young child enters kindergarten, the teenager goes off to college or a job, or the young adult gets married. It is always tempting to want to possess and hold on. It is never easy to let go.

There is a second kind of "letting go" stewardship that is even more difficult. That is a letting go to death.

Sit quietly. Take a moment to remember the last family member's funeral you attended. Think about the person who died and their relationship to you. At the funeral, what were your feelings? How did you feel about that person's dying? How did you feel about God?

Letting go to death is an act of stewardship of the most difficult and radical kind. It is a kind of stewardship which acknowledges that the life of the deceased loved one was never ours to own or to possess in the first place. Letting go to death is a kind of stewardship that remembers that all relationships are a gift from God and that each moment of life spent with the loved one is a privilege.

One of the most helpful books I've ever read on letting go to death is a little book called *Tracks of a Fellow Struggler* by John Claypool. John Claypool is an Episcopal priest who shares, through four sermons preached to his congregation, the way he handled, with God's help, the leukemia and death of his ten-year-old daughter whom he adored. In his book he takes his readers through the personal experience of losing a little girl and helps us to understand that all of life is a gift. He helps us to grasp what this idea of "on loan to love" is all about. He says:

When World War II started, my family did not have a washing machine. With gas rationed and the laundry several miles away, keeping our clothes clean became an intensely practical problem. One of my father's younger business associates was drafted and his wife prepared to go with him, and we offered to let them store their furniture in our basement. Quite unexpectedly, they suggested that we use their washing machine while they were gone.

Since I used to help with the washing, across the years I developed quite an affectionate relationship for that old green Bendix. But eventually the war ended, and our friends returned, and in the meantime I had forgotten how the machine had come to be in our basement in the first place. When they came and took it, I was terribly upset and I said so quite openly.

But my mother . . . said, "Wait a minute, son. You must remember, that machine never belonged to us in the first place. That we ever got to use it at all was a gift. So, instead of being mad at its being taken away, let's use this occasion to be grateful that we had it at all."

Here, in a nutshell, is what it means to understand something as a gift and to handle it with gratitude. I do not mean to say that such a perspective makes things easy, for it does not. But at least it makes things bearable when I remember that [our daughter] was a gift, pure and simple, something I neither earned nor deserved not had a right to. And when I remember that the appropriate response to a gift, even when it is taken away, is gratitude, then I am better able to try and thank God that I was ever given her in the first place.[40]

In all of our relationships, whether raising a child to adulthood and letting go to life, or in witnessing the death of a partner, child, or friend and letting go to death, we can thank God for the gift of life. This is true of all of our loved ones, chosen family or biological family. We can remember that in all our relationships, we do not own or possess other persons. We merely borrow them and cherish them for the time we are given. From the prologue of the Gospel of John we hear: "All things came into being through [God], and without [God] not one thing came into being (John 1:3).

Remind yourself today that you are the steward not only of the land, the mountains, and the seas, but that you are also a steward of people. It is God that hath made us, and not we ourselves (Psalm 100:3). All persons are gifts to us, temporary gifts, created by God, not for us to own or to possess—but merely on loan to love.

MORNING REFLECTION [allow about an hour]

Gather your journal and the photograph you have selected of a loved one and settle into a comfortable place where you can reflect on these questions. Set the photograph before you and use your journal to record your thoughts and feelings.

1. Look at the photo you have brought. How does the idea of "on loan to love" relate to this person?

2. How is "borrowing" a person different from "owning" them?

3. How might this attitude change your approach to your children, your grandchildren, your nieces, your nephews, or any of the young people in your life? How might this attitude change your approach to your spouse or partner or other beloved friends?

4. How are you letting go of or releasing loved ones who have grown up? How are you letting go of or releasing loved ones who have died?

Leader: *Have the journaling questions written on newsprint ahead of time so people can copy them into their journals (or have them printed on handouts). Direct people to take their journals, some art materials, along with the photograph they brought of a love one, to a place where they can quietly respond to the questions. Let them know they will have 40 minutes. Then gather everyone back together by singing a song, if you wish. Divide people into groups of 4, counting off by G-I-F-T, if the numbers come out right. Invite them to share for 20 minutes what is comfortable from their journaling and drawing.*

SONG

Clear your head a bit and sing the verse about the joy of human love in "For the Beauty of the Earth" or sing another song of creation.

For the joy of human love,
brother, sister, parent, child,
Friends on earth, and friends above,
for all gentle thoughts and mild,
God of all, to you we raise
this our hymn of grateful praise.[41]

A PRAYER BEFORE EATING

In the middle of a blank piece of paper, list some elements of God's creation that bring food to your table (such as soil, sun, etc.) At the top of the paper, write, "For these things" and at the bottom of the sheet of paper, write, "I thank you God, Amen." Pray your whole prayer out loud.

Leader: *Follow the directions on the left, substituting a large sheet of newsprint. Have the group brainstorm aloud some elements of God's creation. Add the beginning and end of the prayer as directed, changing "I" to "we." Stand and hold hands in a circle. Pray the prayer in unison.*

LUNCH AND FREE TIME [2 HOURS]

Optional question to ponder during free time:

How am I practicing giving back to God
and caring for all God has created?

If possible, walk outside, absorb the season, notice nature. If you can't go outside, consider relaxing with a new symbol or a new posture. Maybe you could sit in front of a lighted candle or lie on your back on the floor with your arms and legs extended.

afternoon (1 ½ to 2 hours)

centering

Sit with your palms open in a spirit of receptivity.

afternoon meditation

Psalm 139 in Word and Song

Leader: Print on a handout the alternating verses of Psalm 139:1-17 with the words of the song. Invite all to read and sing together. Give the group directions for the accompanying "body prayer" gestures before singing each verse of the song.

THE PSALM: Read out loud.

> *O Lord, you have searched me and known me!*
> *You know when I sit down and when I rise up;*
> * you discern my thoughts from far away.*
> *You search out my path and my lying down,*
> *and are acquainted with all my ways.*
> *Even before a word is on my tongue,*
> *O Lord, you know it completely.*
> *You hem me in behind and before,*
> *and lay your hand upon me.*
> *Such knowledge is too wonderful for me;*
> *it is so high that I cannot attain it.*

THE SONG: The words to this song[42] are set to the melody of "Morning Has Broken." As you sing this verse, cross your hands across your heart, giving thanks to God for having created you.

> *I am the glory.*
> *I am the dwelling.*
> *Incarnation,*
> *Body and Soul.*
> *None other like me,*
> *I am precious.*
> *Gift of creation,*
> *Honored and whole.*

THE PSALM: Read out loud.

> *Where shall I go from your spirit?*
> *Or where shall I flee from your presence?*
> *If I ascend to heaven, you are there;*
> *if I make my bed in Sheol, you are there.*
> *If I take the wings of the morning*
> *and settle at the farthest limits of the sea,*
> *even there your hand shall lead me,*
> *and your right hand shall hold me fast.*
> *If I say, "Surely the darkness shall cover me,*
> *and the light around me become night,"*
> *even the darkness is not dark to you;*
> *the night is as bright as the day,*
> *for darkness is as light to you.*

THE SONG : As you sing this verse, extend your hands out in front of you, to family, friends, loved ones on your mind, giving thanks for their glorious creation.

> *You are the glory.*
> *You are the dwelling.*
> *Incarnation,*
> *Body and Soul.*
> *None other like you,*
> *You are precious.*
> *Gift of creation,*
> *Honored and whole.*

THE PSALM: Read out loud.

> *For it was you who formed my inward parts;*
> *you knit me together in my mother's womb.*
> *I praise you, for I am fearfully and wonderfully made.*
> *Wonderful are your works;*
> *that I know very well.*
> *My frame was not hidden from you,*
> *when I was being made in secret,*

intricately woven in the depths of the earth.
Your eyes beheld my unformed substance.
In your book were written
all the days that were formed for me,
when none of them as yet existed.
How weighty to me are your thoughts, O God!
How vast is the sum of them!

THE SONG: As you sing this verse, raise both arms high above your head, palms open, giving thanks for all whom God has created.

> *We are the glory.*
> *We are the dwelling.*
> *Incarnation,*
> *Body and Soul.*
> *None other like us,*
> *We are precious.*
> *Gift of creation,*
> *honored and whole.*

art as meditation
(allow about 15 minutes)

Read Psalm 139:1-17 again, out loud, listening for images of God's love. Get out your Play-Doh or clay. Close your eyes. Warm the Play-Doh with your hands and soften it up with your fingers. Keeping your eyes closed, form your Play-Doh into one of the images of God's love.[43] Open your eyes and meditate upon what you've made.

Leader: *Hand out Play-Doh or clay to each person. Ask everyone to close their eyes while you read Psalm 139:1-17 again. Ask participants to listen for images of God's love, and with their eyes closed, to form their Play-Doh into one of these images. Remind everyone that this is not an art contest. After 2-3 more minutes, ask everyone to open their eyes and examine what they have made. Invite those who wish to share their images.*

afternoon reflection
(allow about an hour)

Play a quieting piece of music. Then gather your journal and settle into a comfortable place where you can reflect on these questions and record your thoughts and feelings.

1. The meditation shared this morning stated, "We merely borrow our loved ones and cherish them for the time we are given." Are there any relationships you'd like to change? What might you do differently?

2. What relationships in your life are broken? Do not analyze why or make any judgments. Simply place these broken relationships in the Light of God and sit in silence.

3. What person in your life, living or dead, do you miss the most? Take time to reflect.

4. Write a letter to this person. Tell them what they've meant to you. Thank God for their life. (Consider sharing the letter with them if they're still living.)

Leader: *Have the journaling questions written on newsprint ahead of time so people can copy them into their journals (or have them printed on handouts). Direct people to take their journals to a place where they can quietly respond to the questions. Let them know they will have 40 minutes. Then gather everyone back together by singing a song, if you wish. Divide people into groups of 4, counting off by L-O-V-E, if the numbers come out right. Invite them to share for 20 minutes what is comfortable from their journaling.*

closing ritual

SONG: "For the Beauty of the Earth"

For the beauty of the earth,
for the splendor of the skies,
For the love which from our birth
over and around us lies,
God of all, to you we raise
this our hymn of grateful praise.

For the wonder of each hour
of the day and of the night,
Hill and vale, and tree and flower,
sun and moon, and stars of light,
God of all, to you we raise
this our hymn of grateful praise.

For the joy of human love,
brother, sister, parent, child.
Friends on earth, and friends above,
for all gentle thoughts and mild,
God of all, to you we raise
this our hymn of grateful praise.[44]

WRITING YOUR OWN VERSE: Sit and think about what God has given you and what you're thankful for. Don't rush. When you're ready, write a new 4-line verse of "For the Beauty of the Earth" beginning with the words "For the . . ." To finish off your verse, use the refrain, "God of all, to you we raise this our hymn of grateful praise." When you're finished writing, sing your verse of thanksgiving out loud.

Leader: *After each person has written a new verse, invite anyone who wishes to write his or her verse in large letters on newsprint. After the verses have been written on newsprint, sing them together.*

CLOSING PRAYER:

Creating and Bountiful God,
for the joy of human love,
brother, sister, parent, child,
Friends on earth, and friends above,
for all gentle thoughts and mild,
God of all, to you we raise
this our hymn of grateful praise.
Amen.

Leader: *Write this prayer on newsprint so that all may pray it together.*

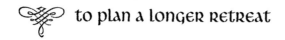 to plan a longer retreat

• SUGGESTION ONE

Roots and Wings

Play a quieting piece of music. Then gather your journal and some art materials, and settle into a comfortable place where you can reflect on these questions and record your thoughts and feelings.

What "roots" were important to you?

What "wings" helped you become who you are today?

How were you given "roots" and "wings?" Draw an image to represent your roots and your wings. Meditate upon your drawing.

How are you offering, or how might you want to offer, roots and wings to others?

Leader: *Have the journaling questions written on newsprint ahead of time so people can copy them into their journals (or have them printed on handouts). Direct people to take their journals and some art materials to a place where they can quietly respond to the questions. Let them know they will have 40 minutes. Then gather everyone back together by singing a song, if you wish. Divide people into groups of 5, counting off by the letters W-I-N-G-S, if the numbers come out right. Invite them to share for 20 minutes what is comfortable from their journaling and drawing.*

• SUGGESTION TWO

Praying with Psalm 104

Read Psalm 104 in its entirety. Be inspired by the psalmist's long recitation of God's majestic works of creation. After thinking about your favorite works of creation, write your own prayer or psalm of thanksgiving using the refrain, "O God, how manifold are your works, in wisdom you have made them all."

Leader: *Invite those who wish to share their prayers or psalms aloud.*

• SUGGESTION THREE

Art As Meditation: Psalm 24:1

Using your art materials and journal, write out the words of Psalm 24:1 in whatever style you wish.

Leader: *Invite any who wish to share their illustrated verse and why they chose to illustrate it in that way.*

*The earth is the Lord's
and all that is in it,
the world,
and those who live in it.*
—Psalm 24:1

Illustrate this verse any way you choose.

• SUGGESTION FOUR.

Scripture and Jewelry-Making

Study Psalm 104, verses 1-4, speaking out loud your favorite phrases and images. Make a pin based on what this biblical poetry is saying to you. (See page 65 for suggested materials). Relax! This is not a test. Have fun.

Leader: *Invite participants to speak aloud their favorite phrases and images. After giving people time to create their pins, invite them to share what they have made and something about what it means to them.*

• SUGGESTION FIVE

Stewardship of the Planet

Set a globe of the earth in front of you.

Psalm 24 tells us:

> *The earth is the Lord's*
> *and all that is in it,*
> *the world,*
> *and those who live in it.*

We know that our planet belongs to God. If a steward is "a person who manages another's property," ponder how you are a steward of the earth.

Use your journal to record your thoughts and feelings about this question:

> *What can I do to care for God's earth?*

Leader: *Set a globe of the earth in the middle of the circle. Read aloud the words on the left. Write the question on newsprint. Record people's answers on the newsprint.*

 SIX.

practicing your call

paying attention to your purpose and vocation

I have called you by name, you are mine.
—Isaiah 43:1b

theme

This retreat provides time to prayerfully consider what God might have in mind for you on this planet. How do you discern your gifts? How do you continue to discover your purpose? How do you do faithfully live into your call from God?

planning ahead

One week before your day of retreat ponder the following questions for reflection and let them simmer as you go about your daily activities:

How would you define call or vocation?

Do you know what your call is?

If so, how has this understanding influenced the way you live your life?

What person do you know who most lives into his or her call?

Before your retreat day, collect the following materials, so you won't be distracted during your retreat:

- journal
- art materials, such as Craypas, markers, or colored pencils
- 2 Bibles (1 for the altar table, 1 for your reading)
- some quieting selections of music to play
- small table on which to create an altar
- white candle and a small plate
- some symbols of work to place on the altar table: a hammer, a computer mouse, a cell phone, a stethoscope, etc.

If you are doing this retreat with a group . . .

———

Leader: *Reflect on these questions for your own preparation. Pray for yourself and each retreat participant.*

Leader: *In addition to asking people bring a journal and a Bible, you will need to supply some the art materials. Also, an easel with newsprint and markers is helpful. Practice reading the guided imagery on page 90 so that you are comfortable with leading it during the retreat.*

- Look over the guided imagery prayer on page 90 and decide whether you want to make, in advance, a tape of yourself reading it aloud or whether you want to read it and pray it when the time comes.
- *Optional:* music for "Amazing Grace"
- *For longer retreats:* you may want to get the video "Tuesdays with Morrie."

CREATING SACRED SPACE

Create an altar by setting a Bible in the middle of a table, with a white candle on a small, safe plate on top of it (but not hiding the title). Light the candle and arrange your selected symbols of work around the Bible.

MORNING (2 to 2 ½ hours)

welcome

Welcome this new day. Stretch your arms toward the sky, inhaling deeply your hopes for this day, exhaling whatever anxieties you wish to put aside. After repeating this several times, consider singing or playing a favorite piece of music to quiet your heart.

Leader: *After leading the group in some stretching and breathing, your welcome should include a description of the day's theme. Suggest a song for the group to sing together or play a quieting piece of music.*

CENTERING

Sit for a few minutes in silence with your hands open on your lap, receptive to God's leading. Breathe in courage. Breathe out unworthiness. Repeat this several times. Prayerfully ponder and review the distractions or obstacles which may be blocking you from receiving this retreat fully. Sit for a few minutes in silence and offer a prayer of invocation asking God's blessing on your retreat.

Leader: *After this time of centering and prayer, allow some time for introductions. If the group is less than twenty, go around the circle sharing the following: "Name one God-given talent that you especially enjoy using." If the group is larger, have people share in smaller groups. (See Appendix B for other Welcoming Suggestions.)*

SCRIPTURE

Read I Samuel 3:1-10.

Now the boy Samuel was ministering to the LORD under Eli. The word of the LORD was rare in those days; visions were not widespread. At that time Eli, whose eyesight had begun to grow dim so that he could not see, was lying down in his room; the lamp of God had not yet gone out, and Samuel was lying down in the temple of the LORD, where the ark of God was. Then the LORD called, "Samuel! Samuel!" and he said, "Here I am!" and ran to Eli, and said, "Here I am, for you called me." But he said, "I did not call; lie down again." So he went and lay down. The LORD called again, "Samuel!" Samuel got up and went to Eli, and said, "Here I am, for you called me." But he said, "I did not call, my son; lie down again." Now Samuel did not yet know the LORD, and the word of the LORD had not yet been revealed to him.

The Lord called Samuel again, a third time. And he got up and went to Eli, and said, "Here I am, for you called me." Then Eli perceived that the LORD was calling the boy. Therefore Eli said to Samuel, "Go, lie down; and if he calls you, you shall say, 'Speak, LORD, for your servant is listening.' " So Samuel went and lay down in his place. Now the Lord came and stood there, calling as before, "Samuel! Samuel!" And Samuel said, "Speak, for your servant is listening."

meditation

Hearing Your Call

Leader: *Present this material in a way that is comfortable for you. Adapt this meditation any way you like, or create your own.*

Most of us who have heard the story about the call of Samuel probably don't remember it very well. When we read the Bible, we tend to recall best those passages that speak to our own lives. At first reading, this story holds little personal appeal. After all, how many of us can truthfully say we have been awakened several times during the night by God's voice? It doesn't happen very often. Samuel's experience may not be our own.

And yet, don't dismiss this intriguing scripture. You may not have been awakened in the night by the voice of God, but I would guess that you have heard God's call somehow and somewhere. Even if you have not received a dramatic summons in the middle of the night, you probably still have some notion of what your call is.

Living into your call: that is what this retreat is all about. Living into your call is one of life's most important spiritual disciplines. What does it mean? Why does it matter?

Perhaps it is easier to think of God's call in terms of vocation. Vocation is a word more familiar to us. The word "vocation" comes from the Latin verb *vocare*, which means "to call." Our call, our vocation, is the thread of purposefulness that runs throughout our lives. The theologian Frederick Buechner defines vocation as "the place where your deep gladness and the world's deep hunger meet."[45] Think about that for a moment: *the place where your deep gladness and the world's deep hunger meet.*

I believe, as Marjory Bankson has said in her book *The Call to the Soul*, that call is not so much a vocational choice but "a special way of understanding what we are here for . . . an invitation to wholeness, a spiritual prompting to complete the work of love that we are here to do."[46] In living out our call, God invites each of us to be our distinctive and precious self. God does not call us to be someone else. God calls us to be only ourselves, in our rich diversity and uniqueness. Teacher and spiritual writer Parker Palmer says,

> I understand vocation . . . not as a goal to be achieved but as a gift to be received. Discovering vocation does not mean scrambling toward some prize just beyond my reach but accepting the treasure of the true self I already possess. Vocation does not come from a voice "out there" calling me to become something I am not. It comes from a voice "in here" calling me to be the person I was born to be, to fulfill the original selfhood given me at birth by God.[47]

Years ago when my husband, John, and I lived in the university community of Iowa City, Iowa, there was a woman known all over town simply as The Elevator Lady. To this day, I have no idea what her real name is. The Elevator Lady was famous, not because she was well-educated or held a high paying job, but simply because she brought joy and cheer into the lives of those around her. The Elevator Lady worked in Mercy Hospital operating the elevator that took the children from the pediatric floor up to surgery. Each day The Elevator Lady would have as her passengers a number of frightened children who were extremely anxious about their upcoming operations. But once on her elevator, the children were talked to, told jokes, giggled with. By the time they got up to surgery, they were smiling and laughing and relaxed.

I share this little story as a reminder of the distinction between job and vocation. The Elevator Lady's *job* was running an elevator at a city hospital. The Elevator Lady's *vocation* was calming frightened children. A person's job and a person's vocation may be one and the same, or they may be different. The important thing is to know what our call is so we can keep our life in balance. When we live from a place of connection with ourselves and with our God, we are living out our sacred purpose. The farther we stray from our God-given purpose or vocation, the more distant we become from our true selves.

Here are the stories of three people who have to make decisions regarding their vocations or calls from God. As you hear these stories, ask yourself: How would I respond to the decisions they have to make?

My name is Rob. I've been a family practice physician for fifteen years. I love my job, and I enjoy getting to know my patients and the details of their lives. But my place of work is in a wealthy, upper-middle-class suburb, and I feel God is calling me to spend my time with more needy people. Our family attends a church here on the North Shore which is a part of a denomination that sends medical missionaries to Africa. The national mission board has asked me if I could sign up for a one-year commitment to help launch a training program. My present place of work will grant me a one-year leave of absence. My wife and my children, five and eleven, will go with me, but they are upset and angry. My wife calls me selfish. Her parents think I've lost my mind and tell me I'm going through a self-absorbed midlife crisis. I would like to go to Africa for just one year. What should I do?

My name is Barbara. I work as an executive secretary at a plastics manufacturing plant. My employer values my years of experience and reimburses me fairly. As far as jobs go, it's a pretty good job, but some days I wonder if there's a point to my work. It is very routine, and in my opinion, not much connected to some higher cause. It is my church that keeps me connected to issues I believe in. It is my church that first encouraged me to do volunteer work. I volunteer two evenings a month at a shelter for homeless women. Every other weekend I spend a day with my young friend in the city as I participate in the Big Brother/Big Sister program. My eleven-year-old friend needs me, and I feel as if I'm making a big difference in her stressful life. At church the other night we had a program on the topic of "call and vocation." All the other people seemed to know right off what their call was, but I'm still confused. My job earns me a living, but it is my volunteer work that makes me feel alive and useful. Can my volunteer work be my call? What do you think?

My name is Emily. I have been a lawyer for almost nine years. I became a lawyer because both of my parents were lawyers who worked primarily with rural African-American fam-

ilies in Alabama. As I grew up in the '60s and '70s, I wanted to make a difference in people's lives, as I saw my mother and father doing. But now I'm working in an office with ferociously competitive and heartless colleagues with whom I have little in common. I long for a kinder, more gentle environment. The bottom line is that my husband, who is a social worker, left me three years ago. Now I'm a single parent, and I need money to support myself and my three young children. I think I've stayed in this office out of inertia, but in sixteen months I'll be vested, which means I will get a respectable pension. The day-to-day stress is killing me, though, and I'm beginning to become a bitter and cynical person. A friend told me there is an opening for a lawyer to head up a nonprofit organization in our city, but the pay is less than half what I'm making now. The cost of living here is high and the support of my children is falling mainly on my shoulders. What should I do?

All through our lives each of us has to make our own choices. Those choices are often challenging and demand significant trade-offs. We all have to come up with the answers that are right for us. You may be grappling with personal decisions about vocation right now. How are you living into your call? What is the thread of purposefulness that runs through your life? What do you see as your vocation?

I am reminded of a little story about a sculptor who was working hard with his hammer and chisel on a large block of marble. A little boy who was watching him saw nothing more than large and small pieces of stone falling away left and right. He had no idea what was happening. But when the boy returned to the studio a few weeks later, he saw to his great surprise a large, powerful lion sitting in the place where the marble had stood. With great excitement the boy ran to the sculptor and said, "Sir, tell me, how did you know there was a lion in that marble?"[48]

The person who seeks to discern God's call is one who knows that there is a lion somewhere in every hunk of marble. One way to recognize the lion is to consider what underlying role we return to play again and again. My husband knows, for example, that even though he is a physician, he will always be, no matter what, a teacher. I know that I will always be a provider of hospitality. A friend of mine who is a pastor and a preacher names herself first a healer.

A call or vocation is not just the privilege of priests, nuns, rabbis, and ministers. God calls laymen and laywomen. God calls anyone with ears to hear. We all have a purpose. We all have to find our "lion." Our lion will show us the way.

MORNING REFLECTION (allow about an hour)

Play a quieting piece of music. Then gather your journal and some art materials, and settle into a comfortable place where you can reflect on the following questions and record your thoughts and feelings.

1. The title of Parker Palmer's book about discovering one's vocation is *Let Your Life Speak*. How are you letting your life speak these days?

2. Is there a "role" you find yourself returning to do again and again, regardless of the particular job you hold? What is your underlying role?

3. How do you see your life as ministry?[49]

Leader: *Have the journaling questions written on newsprint ahead of time so people can copy them into their journals (or have them printed on handouts). Direct people to take their journals and some art materials to a place where they can quietly respond to the questions. Let them know they will have 40 minutes. Then gather everyone back together by singing a song, if you wish. Divide people into groups of 4, counting off by the letters C-A-L-L, if the numbers come out right. Invite them to share for 20 minutes what is comfortable from their journaling and drawing.*

4. Writing an epitaph can shed a great deal of light on understanding your purpose. Here is the epitaph of Maggie Kuhn, the founder of the Gray Panthers:

> *Here lies Maggie Kuhn*
> *Under the only stone she left unturned.* [50]

How would you write your own epitaph?

5. Consider again Frederick Buechner's definition of vocation: *the place where your deep gladness and the world's deep hunger meet.* Using your art materials, illustrate this quotation. Sit and meditate upon your imagery. Then journal your response: Where are you finding "deep gladness" in your life? What does that tell you about your call?

INTERLUDE

Sit quietly and reflect upon those morning when you can hardly wait to jump out of bed. What are you going to do on those days that makes you so eager to get started?

Leader: *Choose a song to sing together before lunch, if you wish.*

A PRAYER BEFORE EATING

God of the Ages, you have called Samuel and Jeremiah and Priscilla and Lydia and me as well. Help me to discover my purpose. Guide me as I embrace my call. Thank you for spiritual food and thank you for food on my plate. Amen.

Leader: *Lead the prayer changing "me" to "us" and "my" to "our." Stand and hold hands in a circle.*

lunch and free time (2 hours)

Optional question to ponder during free time:

How am I living out my God-given purpose?

If possible, walk outside, absorb the season, notice nature. If you can't go outside, consider relaxing with a new symbol or a new posture. Maybe you could sit in front of a lighted candle or lie on your back on the floor with your arms and legs extended.

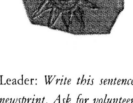

afternoon (1 ½ - 2 hours)

centering

Sit with your palms open in a spirit of receptivity. Say out loud:

"I am the person God created me to be when

_____."

Finish the sentence. Keep repeating this affirmation with a new ending each time until you run out of things to say.

Leader: *Write this sentence on newsprint. Ask for volunteers to finish the sentence out loud.*

guided imagery

A Meditation on Service

Read the following guided imagery prayer very slowly (or play your tape, if you have recorded this imagery in advance). Provide ample time for reflection between phrases.

Leader: *Read the guided imagery very slowly, with plenty of pauses, while participants sit comfortably with their eyes closed.*

Let yourself sit comfortably, being at ease and yet awake. Feel your body sitting and feel the gentle movement of your breath. Let your mind be clear and your heart be soft. Reflect on the bounteous gifts and blessings that support all human life: the rain, the plants of the earth, the warm sunshine. Bring to mind the many human benefactors: the farmers, parents, laborers, healers, postal workers, teachers, the whole society around you. As you feel the world around you, be aware of its problems as well: the needs of its people, its animals, its environment. Let yourself feel the movement in your heart that wishes to contribute, the joy that could come with the offering of your own unique gift to the world.

Then, when you are ready, pose the following questions inwardly to yourself. Pause after each one and give your heart time to answer, allowing a response from the deepest level of your compassion and wisdom.

Imagine yourself five years from now as you would most like to be, having done all the things you want to have done, having contributed all the things you want to contribute in the most heartfelt way.

What is your greatest source of happiness? {Pause}

What is the thing you've done by which you feel the world is most blessed? {Pause}

What is the contribution you could make to the world that would give you the most satisfaction? {Pause}

To make this contribution to the world, what unworthiness would you have to relinquish? {Pause}

To make this contribution to the world, what strengths and capacities would you have to recognize in yourself and others? {Pause}

What would you have to do in your life today to begin this service, this contribution? {Pause}

Why not begin? . . . [51]

Open your eyes and slowly focus your attention back in this room.

JOURNALING (allow about 15 minutes)

Record your thoughts and feelings about this guided imagery in your journal.

Leader: *Give people 5-10 minutes to share with a partner their response to the guided imagery.*

meditation

A Personal Rule

Leader: *Adapt this meditation in a way that is comfortable for you. Adapt this meditation in any way you like, or create your own.*

A personal rule is a set of ethical guidelines that a person aspires to live and grow into. A personal rule is a statement of intention, a mission statement of one's life. The ultimate example of a personal rule is the Rule of St. Benedict, written in sixth-century Italy, which continues to be the code of spiritual conduct for Benedictine communities around the world today.

A personal rule serves as a kind of plumb line by which to gauge your actions and conduct. Creating a personal rule can help you connect your call to your everyday actions. Personal rules vary as widely as the individuals who write them. Here are some examples.

A personal rule of the third-century desert father St. Anthony:
- Whoever you may be, always have God before your eyes.
- Whatever you do, do it according to the testimony of the holy scriptures.
- Whatever place you live, do not easily leave it.[52]

A personal rule for membership in The Church of the Saviour in Washington, D.C.:
- To spend one hour a day in prayer, meditation, and devotional reading.
- To worship with my gathered community once a week.
- To participate in a mission group that is responsive to the claims of the poor.
- To tithe my gross income as a basis for "proportional" sharing of my livelihood.[53]

A personal rule of Martin Luther King, Jr.'s nonviolent civil rights demonstrators:
- Meditate daily on the teachings and life of Jesus.
- Remember always that the nonviolent movement in Birmingham seeks justice and reconciliation—not victory.
- Walk and talk in the manner of love, for God is love.
- Pray daily to be used by God in order that all people might be free.
- Sacrifice personal wishes in order that all people might be free.
- Observe with both friend and foe the ordinary rules of courtesy.
- Seek to perform regular service for others and for the world.
- Refrain from violence of fist, tongue, or heart.
- Strive to be in good spiritual and bodily health.
- Follow the directions of the movement and the demonstration's captain.[54]

A personal rule of Donna Schaper, United Church of Christ pastor and author:
- To meditate on the word "enough."
- To make a Sabbath effort to play at my work and to work at my play.
- To connect my inner life to my outer life.
- To meditate on the meaning of the Christian creed that promises the resurrection of the body and life everlasting. To consider the paradox of becoming more youthful over time.
- To try to understand the sacrament of marriage as deeply as I can: as a nest and hope for my family and my deepest personal connection to others.[55]

---

afternoon reflection
(allow about 40 minutes)

Gather your journal and settle into a comfortable place. Write a personal rule. Consider the following questions to help you think about what you want to include:

Leader: *Have the journaling questions written on newsprint ahead of time so people can copy them into their journals (or have them printed on handouts). Direct people to take their journals to a place where they can quietly respond to the questions. Let them know they will have 25 minutes.*

- What kinds of values and ideas have you been embracing these last few years?

- How comfortable are you with them?

- Are there any new guidelines you would like to add or adopt for yourself?

Remember there is no right way to write a personal rule. Personal rules vary a great deal from one person to another. See what appears.

Then gather everyone back together by singing a song, if you wish. Divide people into groups of 4, counting off by the letters R-U-L-E, if the numbers come out right. Invite them to share for 15 minutes what is comfortable from their personal rules.

CLOSING RITUAL

SONG: Sing the following song to the tune of "Amazing Grace." (Extend your arms out in front of you with your palms open.)

Leader: *Have everyone join hands in a circle as they sing.*

> My gifts to God are rich indeed,
> Unique to me alone.
> God's call and purpose forward lead,
> Through me God's seeds are sown.[56]

BLESSING: Stand, as you are able, and cross your arms on your chest. Bless yourself with the words, "I am called and loved by God."

SONG: Sing the preceding song once more.

Leader: *Stand and gather in a circle, pairing off. (If there is an odd number, one group of three can stand together). Bless one another with the words, "You are called and loved by God."*

• SUGGESTION ONE

How Will You Be Remembered? [57]

Write your obituary, completing the following sentences;

(Name), age _____, died yesterday from . . .

He/She was a member of . . .

He/She is survived by . . .

At the time of his/her death she was working on becoming . .

He/She will be remembered for . . .

He/She will be mourned by _____ because . . .

His/Her community will suffer the loss of her contribution in the areas of . . .

He/She always wanted, but never got to . . .

In lieu of flowers, send . . .

Leader: *After participants have had time in solitude to write their obituaries, gather people in small groups to discuss these questions: What did you learn from writing your obituaries? Did anything surprise you?*

• SUGGESTION TWO

Bible Study

Read these two passages about the call of Jeremiah and the call of Moses:

Jeremiah 1:4-10 (The call of Jeremiah)
Exodus 3:1-12 (The call of Moses)

Use your journal to consider to this question:

*How is your call the same or different
from the call of Jeremiah and the call of Moses?*

Leader: *Divide the larger group into six small groups and assign one of the following Bible passage to each group. Ask for a volunteer note taker from each group who will be willing to summarize the group's discussion a bit later*

- *Jeremiah 1:4-10
  (The call of Jeremiah)*
- *Exodus 3:1-12
  (The call of Moses)*
- *Matthew 4:18-22
  (The call of Peter, Andrew, James and John)*
- *Romans 12:3-8
  (The body has many members, differing gifts)*
- *I Corinthians 12:1-11
  (A variety of spiritual gifts)*
- *II Corinthians 5:16-17
  (We become new in Christ)*

Write the following instructions on newsprint:

- *Have someone in the group read the passage slowly aloud.*
- *Meditate in silence for about three minutes.*
- *Discuss: What does the passage say about vocation and call?*
- *Discuss: How does the passage speak to you personally?.*

After each group has had Bible study time, invite each group to report back to the large group on how their particular scripture spoke to them.

• SUGGESTION THREE

Some Thoughts On Vocation

Read each of these quotations aloud and consider, in your journal, what each quotation means in the context of your life.

> *"Vocation essentially is about who we are and what we are called to become."*

> *"Vocation is the recognition that God has a claim on our lives and calls us to participate in the continuing transformation of the world."*

> *"A calling is made possible by intellectual and personal gifts shaped by historical moment and the crossing of self and society."* [58]

Leader: *Write these quotations on newsprint one by one and discuss one at a time.*

• SUGGESTION FOUR

Go back to the "Hearing Your Call" meditation on pages 85-86 and find the stories of Rob, Barbara, and Emily. Spend some time journaling about how you would respond in each situation.

Leader: *Give people time after each to discuss in small groups or pairs how they would respond.*

• SUGGESTION FIVE

Movie! Movie!

When you need to stop your deep introspection and do something else, get out the video "Tuesdays with Morrie" based on Mitch Albom's bestseller and starring Jack Lemmon and Hank Azaria. Think about how this movie relates to call and purposefulness.

Leader: *After viewing the movie, lead a discussion on how this film relates to call and purposefulness.*

 seven.

practicing accountability

nurturing routines
to keep faithful

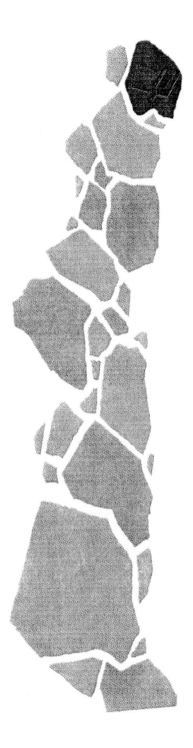

When we structure spiritual interludes into our day, we are giving spiritual forces the chance to re-create us, to make us over in a better mold. We open ourselves to receive guidance and to experience contact with the divine.[59]
—Julia Cameron, *Some People Say That God Is No Laughing Matter*

theme

This retreat explores spiritual accountability. How can you nurture your spiritual life for the long haul? What practices will enable you to live with integrity and faithfulness?

planning ahead

One week before your day of retreat, ponder the following question for reflection and let it simmer as you go about your daily activities:

When you think of spiritual accountability, what comes to mind?

Before your retreat day, collect the following materials, so you won't be distracted during your retreat:

- journal
- art materials, such as Craypas, markers, or colored pencils
- Bible
- some quieting selections of music to play
- small table on which to create an altar
- white candle
- some objects or symbols that call you back to spiritual accountability (perhaps the Bible or a rosary or a prayer book or a family picture)
- an index card
- a gray lake or river stone, along with gold or silver metallic markers
- *Optional:* music for "I Love to Tell the Story" and "Jesus Loves Me"

If you are doing this retreat with a group . . .

Leader: *Study the five ways presented in this retreat for keeping spiritually accountable. Which of these do you practice? What other ways would you add to the list? Consider teaching about these, also, drawing from your own experience. Finally, consider who supports you in your accountability. Pray for yourself and each retreat participant.*

Leader: *In addition to asking people bring a journal and a Bible, you will need to supply some art materials. Also, an easel with newsprint and markers is helpful. You may also want to collect some recordings of old Gospel hymns to set the mood at the beginning of the retreat. Look over the closing ritual carefully. You will need an index card and a gray lake or river stone for each participant, along with a supply of gold and silver metallic pens.*

CREATING SACRED SPACE

Create an altar table by lighting a white candle and surrounding it with the symbols you have gathered that call you to spiritual accountability.

MORNING (2 to 2 ½ hours)

WELCOME

Welcome this new day. Stretch your arms toward the sky, inhaling deeply your hopes for this day, exhaling whatever anxieties you wish to put aside. After repeating this several times, consider singing or playing a favorite piece of music to quiet your heart.

Leader: *If appropriate to your setting, play recordings of old Gospel hymns while people are gathering.*

Leader: *After leading the group in some stretching and breathing, your welcome should include a description of the day's theme. Suggest a song for the group to sing together or play a quieting piece of music.*

CENTERING

Sit for a few minutes in silence with your hands in your lap, receptive to God's leading. Breathe in purposefulness. Breathe out confusion. Repeat this several times. Prayerfully ponder and review the distractions or obstacles which may be blocking you from receiving this retreat fully. Pass these over to God's loving care. Sit for a few minutes in silence and offer a prayer of invocation asking God's blessing on your retreat.

Leader: *After this time of centering and prayer, allow some time for introductions. If the group is less than twenty, go around the circle answering the question: "What nourishes your spiritual life the most?" If the group is larger, have people share in smaller groups. (See Appendix B for other Welcoming Suggestions.)*

meditation &
reflection 1
(allow about 20-30 minutes)

Leader: *In this retreat there are five "accountability meditations," each followed by a set of journaling questions. Present the meditations in a way that is comfortable for you. Write the reflection questions on newsprint. Choose, or alternate, or combine any of the following: (a) discuss as a large group; (b) break into smaller groups for discussion; (c) invite people to journal privately.*

Practicing Accountability
through Worship

Most of our lives are hectic and demanding. We adhere to tight schedules while being bombarded by the needs of our children, our parents, our co-workers, and our friends.

We dwell in a driven "buy, buy, buy" society where we are tempted to believe that who we are is what we own. To remember who we are, and *whose* we are, we need to live with some amount of attentiveness and some amount of accountability. Casinos and bingo halls often post the sign: "You must be present to win." The question for us is how can we live as spiritual winners? How can we be present to our deeper selves?

Several years ago my husband and I were cleaning out our basement and were ecstatic to discover a seventy-five-year-old Shinto temple bell that John's missionary grandmother had brought home from Japan. After cleaning it up a bit, we tested it out. When struck, this temple bell has a remarkable resonance, similar to the now popular Tibetan singing bowls. Its deep, clear reverberations now echo frequently throughout our house.

Our spiritual lives reverberate in the same way . . . when we are faithful and when we are accountable. There are five actions that can help us stay accountable:

- worshiping in a faith community
- going on retreat
- reading the Bible
- meeting regularly with a spiritual director
- keeping ourselves steady with a daily inventory or examination of conscience

When it comes to worship, I'm not one that buys the line, "I can just as easily worship God out on the golf course." I like to play golf, too, but I sure can tell the difference between a game of golf and going to church. Communal worship stretches us, challenges us, comforts us, and connects us. We read in the Gospel of Matthew: "For where two or three are gathered in my name, I am there among them" (Matthew 12:20). When we go to church, we know that we are part of a community. When we sing hymns together, when we participate in intercessory prayer, when we share our faith stories in Sunday school or Bible study, we know that we are not alone. We experience the undergirding of mutual support and the kinship of those who depend on God's grace.

The hilarious and often poignant author Anne Lamott has a chapter in her spiritual autobiography, *Traveling Mercies,* called "Why I Make Sam Go to Church." When she writes about why she wants her young son to be a part of a faith community she says:

> The main reason is that I want to give him what I found in the world, which is to say a path and a little light to see by. Most of the people I know who have what I want—which is to say, purpose, heart, balance, gratitude, joy—are people with a deep sense of spirituality. They are people in community, who pray, or practice their faith. They follow a brighter light than the glimmer of their own candle; they are part of something beautiful. I saw something once from the Jewish Theological Seminary that said, "A human life is like a single letter of the alphabet. It can be meaningless. Or it can be a part of a great meaning." Our funky little church is filled with people who are working for peace and freedom, who are out there on the streets and inside praying, and they are home writing letters, and they are at the shelters with giant platters of food.[60]

Worshiping with a faith community helps us to be a part of something larger than ourselves.

Reflect in your journal on these questions:
What is "church" to you?
What is worship to you?
What do you give to your faith community?
What do you get from your faith community?

meditation & reflection 2 (allow 20-30 minutes)

Practicing Accountability
by Going on Retreat

Retreats offer us an opportunity to ponder our relationship with ourselves, our loved ones, and with God in a place away. Mark 6 tell us:

> The apostles gathered around Jesus, and told him all that they had done and taught. He said to them, "Come away to a deserted place all by yourselves and rest a while." For many were coming and going, and they had no leisure even to eat. And they went away in the boat to a deserted place by themselves. (Mark 6:30-32)

Retreats offer us a respite from that which is overly familiar and routine. The dictionary defines "retreat" as "the act of withdrawing" or "a place of refuge."[61] On retreat, we have a chance to stand back and to regard our lives from a fresh perspective. Along with that fresh perspective come new inspirations and new resolves.

Retreats abound. There are silent retreats, preached retreats, experiential retreats. They can be a day long or a month long or anything in between. Getting away overnight for at least a day or two can be particularly helpful.

Retreats are marvelously and unpredictably renewing. The Holy Spirit often speaks to us on retreat because it is there, particularly, that we are vulnerable and available and open. Consider becoming familiar with the retreats being offered by your own church or denomination or at the conference centers, colleges, convents, or monasteries near your home. Make some calls. Get on some mailing lists.

Author Macrina Wiederkehr suggests a retreat day, a day of "loving examination," on our date of birth each month.[62] If your birthday were the 8th of June, for example, then the 8th of each month could be your monthly retreat day. Try committing yourself to a day of reflection every month or several overnight retreats each year.

Reflect in your journal on these questions:
What is a "retreat" to you?
How does having time and space apart affect you?
What commitment to "retreating" would you like to make for yourself?

meditation & reflection 3 (allow about an hour)

Practicing Accountability
by Reading Scripture

Whether you memorized Bible verses as a child, or hear the Bible read every week at church, or are considering reading it for the first time, I have one piece of advice: Don't imagine what the Bible has to tell you; find out for yourself.

Admittedly, if studying the Bible is new for you, it can seem daunting at first. A good way to start is to ask if your denomination or community of faith publishes a devotional booklet with a brief scripture reading and a short meditation for each day. This is an excellent way to get to know the parts of the Bible.

Here are some other ideas about ways to approach Scripture:

- Read the Psalms. They are passionate: loving, rageful, and everything in between. They tell of persons whose relationship with God is honest and intimate. You may find yourself repeating phrases that just won't leave your heart.

- Purchase a children's Bible or Bible story book for yourself to read. Two favorites on my bookshelf are *The Crossroad Children's Bible* and *Bible Stories for Children* retold by Geoffrey Horn and Arthur Cavanaugh and published by Macmillan.

- Enroll in a Bible study class at your church or community of faith or local college or seminary with a qualified teacher whom you respect and who is open to dialogue.

- Buy a Bible with a good commentary. In seminary circles, the *New Oxford Annotated Bible of the New Revised Standard Version (NRSV)* is highly regarded and is extremely helpful with interpretive notes at the bottom of each page. Another user-friendly resource compiled by a group of well-respected scholars is the *Spiritual Formation Bible* (Zondervan) which includes suggestions for deepening one's spiritual life on each page.

- Find a book that puts the Bible in context and will help you understand the whole picture. One favorite of mine is Walter Brueggemann's *The Bible Makes Sense.* Other titles include Peter J. Gomes' *The Good Book,* Marcus Borg's *Reading the Bible Again for the First Time*, and Thomas Cahill's *The Gifts of the Jews* and *Desire of the Everlasting Hills.*

Reflect on these questions in your journal:
What is your perception of, or experience, with the Bible? As a child? As an adult?
What role does the Bible have—or would you like it to have—in your life today?
How could you become more familiar with the Bible?

SONG

If you wish, sing "Jesus Loves Me" or another old favorite you know by heart.

BIBLE STUDY (LECTIO DIVINA)

One of the oldest and most familiar methods of Bible study is called *lectio divina* or divine reading. This simply means reading and praying with the scripture. The classical form of *lectio divina* has four parts: reading *(lectio)*, meditation *(meditatio)*, prayer *(oratio)*, and contemplation *(contemplatio)*. True *lectio* might be called "hearing with your heart." The process is like peeling layers off an onion, revealing a new essentialness each time. Through repetition, we become more and more present to the scripture as well as to ourselves.

Choose a passage for your Bible study. You might want to select one of the readings from the lectionary for next Sunday, or page through the Gospel of Mark until you come to a story or parable that sounds familiar. Have your journal handy.

Leader: *Divide the large group into small groups of 5 or 6 people. Write group instructions for* Lectio Divina *(see next page) on newsprint or create a handout.*

READING (lectio)

Read the scripture out loud. Listen for words or phrases that capture your attention. Take a moment of silence.

MEDITATION (meditatio)

Read the scripture out loud again. Listen for sensory messages: *What sights? What sounds? What smells? What tastes? What textures?*

Take a moment of silence. Then read the scripture silently to yourself. *What do you find yourself thinking about as you read this passage? What ideas emerge?*

PRAYER (oratio)

Read the scripture out loud again. Consider how this passage relates to your experience.

> *What might God be asking of you?*
> *What do you want to ask of God?*

Take several minutes to write a brief prayer. Pray your prayer aloud. Take a moment of silence.

CONTEMPLATION (contemplatio)

Read the scripture aloud one (last!) time. Sit quietly. Imagine that you are climbing into the lap of the Divine Presence to seek comfort and peace. Do not strive for anything. For several minutes, just sit quietly and be.

CLOSING PRAYER (lectio divina)

> *Thanks be to you, O Holy One, for the wisdom and the nourishment of scripture. Amen.*

Leader: *Have one person read the scripture aloud. Go around your group sharing responses without additional comment.*

Leader: *Have another person read the scripture aloud. Then share responses without additional comment.*

Ask each person to read the scripture silently. Then share responses aloud without additional comment.

Leader: *Have another person read the scripture aloud. After considering in silence the two questions, allow several minutes for each person to write a brief prayer. Invite people to share their prayer aloud, without additional comment. (Anyone is free to pass.)*

Leader: *Have another person read the scripture aloud, one last time. After that person has finished reading, sit quietly.*

Leader: *Call the small groups together into the large group once more. Write this prayer on newsprint. Invite everyone to pray it together.*

song

Sing "Jesus Loves Me" one more time.

a prayer before eating

Most Holy One, you nourish me
*   with your unconditional love.*
Most Holy One, you nourish me
*   with promises you have kept.*
Most Holy One, you nourish me
*   with food each day.*
Most Holy One,
*   I give you thanks and praise.*
Amen.

Leader: *Write the prayer on newsprint changing "me" to "us" and "I" to "we." Stand and hold hands in a circle. Pray in unison or have participants repeat the prayer line by line after you.*

lunch and free time [2 hours]

Optional question to ponder during free time:

What practices or what people help me to keep accountable in living a satisfying spiritual life?

If possible, walk outside, absorb the season, notice nature. If you can't go outside, consider relaxing with a new symbol or a new posture. Maybe you could sit in front of a lighted candle or lie on your back on the floor with your arms and legs extended.

afternoon [1 ½ to 2 hours]

centering

Sit with your palms open in a spirit of receptivity. Hum a favorite hymn.

meditation & Reflection 4 [allow about 20-30 minutes]

Practicing Accountability
by Meeting with a Spiritual Director

A spiritual director or spiritual friend is a companion with whom you meet regularly to talk about the perceived presence or absence of God in your life. The ancient practice of spiritual direction is an ongoing relationship in which a person who wishes to be attentive to his or her spiritual life meets with another person, usually once a month for an hour.

A good opening spiritual direction question can be borrowed from the poet William Wordsworth: "Tell me, what has come clear to you since last we met?"[63]

Rose Mary Dougherty, faculty member at the Shalem Institute for Spiritual Formation, likes to quote an African Proverb when defining the spiritual direction relationship: "It is because one antelope will blow the dust from the other's eyes that two antelopes walk together." A spiritual director listens to us with empathy, cares for us, prays for us, and helps us to sort out divine stirrings amidst the substance of our lives, always asking: *Where is God in all this?* A spiritual director is a midwife or stagehand ushering in an awareness of God's activity and guidance.

If you are thinking you would like some consistent companionship on your spiritual journey, consider meeting regularly with a spiritual friend. Here are some suggestions about what to look for in a spiritual director:

- a person who is spiritually mature yet does not pretend to have all the answers.
- a person who relies on the grace of God.
- a person who is a perceptive and attentive listener who holds in confidence your sacred story.
- a person who nurtures his or her own spiritual life.
- a person who will hold you in prayer.

Reflect in your journal on the following questions:

IF YOU HAVE MET WITH A SPIRITUAL DIRECTOR BEFORE:
What was the experience like for you?
Is there anything in your life at present around which you would like spiritual guidance?
How might meeting with a spiritual director each month provide you some support?

IF YOU HAVEN'T MET WITH A SPIRITUAL DIRECTOR BEFORE:
Are there some areas in your life around which you would like some spiritual guidance?
How might meeting with a spiritual director each month provide you some support?

---

song

Stop and sing a song such as "I Love to Tell the Story" before moving on to the next meditation.

meditation & reflection 5 [allow about a half hour]

Practicing Accountability with a Daily Inventory

Search me, O God, and know my heart;
test me and know my thoughts.
—Psalm 139:23

I am a parent of teenage children, a clergywoman, a wife, a spiritual director, a retreat leader, a cook, a soccer mom, and a school volunteer. And sometimes I don't cope very well with the stress of it all. I rely on a daily inventory to add sanity, stability, and a sense of reconnection with God's grace.

The awareness examen or inventory (known by various names in the Christian tradition, such as examination of conscience, examination of consciousness) is an ancient and reputable spiritual tool that serves to keep us accountable to ourselves and to God. Such historical figures as Seneca, Phythagoras, Antony of the Desert, Chrysostom, and Basil all advocated use of the examen. The practice experienced a resurgence of popularity through St. Ignatius of Loyola (1495-1556) in his Spiritual Exercises.

The awareness examen, the daily inventory I have created for myself, offers me a framework for reflection and prayer twice a day, once in the morning and once at night. It goes like this:

Morning Questions to Start the Day
What is my intention for this day?
How do I wish to conduct myself?
How might God be asking me to let go?
Where do I seek God's wisdom and guidance?

Evening Questions to End the Day
What have been my sources of grace for this day?
For what do I give thanks?
For what do I repent?

I rely on the fact that my daily inventory is flexible and that I can omit certain questions or add pertinent new ones at any time. Last week, for example, I added a fourth question to my morning inventory: "What is God inviting me into?"

You may want to reflect on your own spiritual challenges and create your own daily inventory. It is an insightful tool that has worked well for me.

---

afternoon reflection
(allow about 45 minutes)

Play a quieting piece of music. Then gather your journal and settle into a comfortable place where you can reflect on these questions and record your thoughts and feelings.

1. Think about how you start your morning. What questions might you ask yourself that would focus your attention on your spiritual growth in the day ahead.

Leader: *Have the journaling questions written on newsprint ahead of time so people can copy them into their journals (or have them printed on handouts). Direct people to take their journals to a place where they can quietly respond to the questions. Let them know they will have 30 minutes.*

Jot these down under the heading "Morning Questions to Start the Day."

2. Think about what the end of your day is like. What questions would help you understand the spiritual challenges of the day and help you reconnect with God's grace. Jot these down under the heading "Evening Questions to End the Day."

3. Sit and prayerfully ponder how you want to use these questions.

Leader: *Gather everyone back together by singing a song, if you wish. Divide people into groups of 5, counting off by the letters D-A-I-L-Y, if the numbers come out right. Invite them to share for 15 minutes what is comfortable from their journaling.*

Closing Ritual

INTENTION: This retreat has presented various options for nourishing your spirit. Which practices seem best for you at this time and at this stage of your life? Consider and complete the following sentence:

"I will nourish my spiritual life by

_____.*"*

Finish this sentence on an index card that you can put somewhere in your home where you will see it: on the refrigerator door, on the bathroom mirror, on your computer monitor, etc.

Create a paperweight for yourself as a tangible reminder of accountability. Using a gold or silver metallic pen, write your spiritual intentions on a gray lake or river stone. Keep it in a place where you will be reminded of your intentions.

Leader: *Write this sentence on newsprint. Ask each person to think about how they would finish the sentence. Hand out index cards, stones, and metallic marking pens.*

After participants have completed their cards and paperweights, gather everyone in a circle, holding hands. Invite anyone who wishes to share their intentions aloud saying, "I will nourish my spiritual life by _____." (You may want to set an example and go first.)

PRAYER:

Holy and Sustaining God,
I pray for my intention
to nurture my spiritual life,
and to live as a faithful Christian.
Support me in my resolve.
Comfort me, guide me,
and strengthen me, I pray. Amen.

SONG: If you want, sing "This Little Light of Mine" or another favorite about the spiritual life.

Leader: *Lead this prayer, changing "I" to "we" and "my" to "our."*

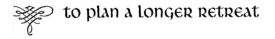 to plan a longer retreat

• SUGGESTION ONE

A Personal Rule

If there is time and you haven't done it before, by all means include the exercise of writing a "personal rule" as part of this retreat on "Practicing Accountability." See the background information and examples in the "Practicing Your Call" retreat on pages 91-93.

• SUGGESTION TWO

Living Intentionally

Create a new retreat called "Living Intentionally: Vocation, Purpose, and Accountability" by combining this "Practicing Accountability" retreat and the "Practicing Your Call" retreat on page 79 together into one longer weekend retreat. The theme of the new retreat could be described in the following way.

Living Intentionally:
Vocation, Purpose, and Accountability

THEME: As we embrace this first half of the twenty-first century, it is a particularly apt time to prayerfully consider what God might have in mind for each of us on this planet. This retreat will help to answer the questions: How do we discern our gifts? How do we continue to discover our vocation? How do we live with intentionality, faithfulness, and accountability?

❧ appendix a.
end-of-series
celebration

If you have experienced all or most of the retreats in this book, you may want to plan a longer closing for your last retreat, whatever one that happens to be. Consider your own personality and your own spiritual path. Think about whether you would like to put together a closing celebration. Gather sufficient supplies. A suggested time for this review and ritual is forty-five minutes to an hour.

If you are doing this celebration with a group . . .

Leader: *Ask your retreat participants ahead of time if they would enjoy taking part in a closing celebration of this kind. If you decide to plan this, reflect on what supplies or props would be helpful for this experience. You may want to ask others for help in bringing what you need. A suggested time for this review and ritual is 1 ½ to 2 hours.*

questions for reflection

What will you take away from these retreats?

What do you remember most?

What will continue to help you live an intentional life?

Leader says: *"We have been together now on (number of) retreats as we have explored spiritual practices and have shared the stories of our lives. We have collectively practiced our paths and learned Christian principles that will help us live out an intentional life." Write the questions on newsprint and invite people to share their responses.*

A CREATIVE OFFERING [64]

*What can you create
to express what you have learned?*

Choose a medium of expression:

- a piece of music
- a movement
- a liturgy or ritual
- a poem
- a piece of art

Give yourself enough time to let your thoughts and feelings reveal themselves in a creative form.

THE SHARING: When you're finished, share your creation with God as an act of thanksgiving.

CLOSING PRAYER: End your celebration in any way you see fit or offer a closing prayer aloud to God.

Leader says: "We're going to be planning a closing celebration that will give us an opportunity to bring together what we have learned. We will need everyone's gifts and participation." Write the question on newsprint, along with these five signs:

- *One group will create a piece of music.*
- *One group will create a movement.*
- *One group will create a liturgy or ritual.*
- *One group will create a poem.*
- *One group will create a piece of art.*

Leader says: "There are signs posted around the room (or, ideally, in a larger facility each group can go to a separate room) for different creative options. Think about what group you would like to be a part of and go to that place now. After 45 minutes, come back and each group will present its offering for the larger group as a thanksgiving to God."

appendix B.

welcoming suggestions for a group leader

- Give participants permission to do whatever their souls require during the day, even if it means departing from the group's agenda.

- Go over the schedule and offer directions to bathrooms, coat racks, breakout rooms, dining room, nature trails, etc.

- During the time of introductions and community-building, you may want to ask each person and put on newsprint:

  What is your name?

  Where are you from?

  Is there anything else about yourself you'd like us to know?

- Additional Icebreakers or Community-Building Suggestions:[65]

  Where did your name come from? What association do you have with your name?

  Speak aloud an encouraging message you wish you had received as child.

  Share a word or a symbol of your daily work.

  Describe a new behavior or choice you are making, no matter how small it may be.

  What sign of your major commitments do you wear or have in your home?

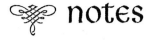 # notes

one: practicing sabbath

1. Thich Nhat Hanh, *Peace Is Every Step* (New York: Bantam, 1992), 39.
2. Wayne Muller, *Sabbath: Restoring the Sacred Rhythm of Rest* (New York: Bantam, 1999), 211.
3. Tilden H. Edwards, *Spiritual Friend: Reclaiming the Gift of Spiritual Direction* (New York: Paulist Press, 1980), 69.
4. Donna Schaper, *Sabbath Sense: A Spiritual Antidote for the Overworked* (Philadelphia: Innisfree Press, 1997), 14.
5. *Ibid.*, 79.
6. Flexner, ed. *The Random House Dictionary of the English Language, Second Edition, Unabridged*, 1987.
7. Schaper, *Sabbath Sense,* 52, 14, 63, 119, 79, respectively.
8. Muller, *Sabbath*, 36.
9. *The New Century Hymnal* (Cleveland: Pilgrim Press, 1995), hymn 502.
10. This letter, in the form of spiritual direction correspondence, was written to "Elizabeth," a pseudonym, and is reprinted with her permission.
11. Denise Levertov, *Oblique Prayers* (New York: New Directions, 1984), 76.
12. Idea from Donna Schaper at the "Sabbath Living" retreat, Green Lake Conference Center, Green Lake, Wisconsin, 13-14 November 1998.
13. Adapted from the *Pilgrim Hymnal* (New York: Pilgrim Press, 1986), hymn 395.

two: practicing hospitality

14. Marjorie J. Thompson, *Soul Feast: An Invitation to the Christian Spiritual Life* (Louisville: Westminster John Knox, 1995), 120-121.
15. Timothy Fry, O.S.B., ed., *The Rule of St. Benedict in English* (Collegeville: Minnesota: The Liturgical Press, 1982), 73.
16. Thich Nhat Hanh, *Present Moment Wonderful Moment* (Berkeley: Parallax Press, 1990), 48.

17. This story is taken from three sources: Theodore Knight, *The Olympic Games* (San Diego: Lucent Books, 1991), 64-67; Jesse Owens with Paul G. Niemark, *Blackthink: My Life as Black Man and White Man* (New York: William Morrow and Company, Inc., 1970), 183-193. The bracketed quotations indicate more comprehensible translations of Luz Long's English words; Robert Sandelson, *Olympic Sports: Track Athletics* (New York: Macmillan Publishing Company, 1991), 13-14.

18. Owens, *Blackthink*, 185.

19. *Ibid.*, 187.

20. *Ibid.*, 191.

21. *Ibid.*, 192-193.

22. Bonni Goldberg, *Room to Write* (New York: Jeremy P. Tarcher/Putnam, 1996), 56.

three: practicing prayer and action

23. Tilden Edwards, *Living in the Presence: Disciplines for the Spiritual Heart* (San Francisco: Harper & Row, 1987), 11.

24. Maria Harris, *Dance of the Spirit: The Seven Steps of Women's Spirituality* (New York: Bantam Books: 1989), 137.

25. Douglas V. Steere, "Intercession: Caring for Souls," *Weavings* 4, no. 2 (March/April 1989): 22.

26. As cited by Jane Redmont in *When In Doubt, Sing: Prayer in Daily Life* (New York: HarperCollinsPublishers, 1999), 382.

27. Holly W. Whitcomb, *Feasting with God* (Cleveland: United Church Press, 1996), 45-46.

28. Joseph Campbell with Bill Moyers, *The Power of Myth* (New York: Doubleday, 1988), 32.

29. This LEGO exercise is adapted from Drew Leder, *Games for the Soul* (New York: Hyperion, 1998), 104-107.

30. Redmont, *When in Doubt, Sing*, 267.

31. *The New Century Hymnal,* hymn 591.

32. As quoted by M. J. Ryan (ed.) in *A Grateful Heart* (Berkeley, Conari Press, 1994), 29.

33. *The Canticles* from *The Liturgical Psalter* (Chicago: Liturgy Training Publications, 1995), 92.

four: practicing the fast

34. Thompson, *Soul Feast*, 76.

35. *Ibid.* Thompson poses this question in her excellent chapter on feasting, 69-81.

36. Edwards, *Living in the Presence*, 31.

37. Thompson, *Soul Feast*, 74.

38. Mitch Albom, *Tuesdays with Morrie* (New York: Doubleday, 1997), 125.

39. As quoted by Muller in *Sabbath*, 179.

five: practicing giving back to god

40. John Claypool, *Tracks of a Fellow Struggler: How to Handle Grief* (Waco, Texas: World Books, 1974), 75-76.

41. *The New Century Hymnal*, hymn 28.

42. Lyrics by Holly Whitcomb.

43. Thanks to Cil Braun of Minneapolis for sharing this idea.

44. *The New Century Hymnal*, hymn 28.

six: practicing your call

45. Frederick Buechner, *Wishful Thinking: A Seeker's ABC* (San Francisco: HarperSanFrancisco, 1993), 119.

46. Marjory Zoet Bankson, *The Call to the Soul: Six Stages of Spiritual Development* (Philadelphia: Innisfree Press), 1999, 19.

47. Parker J. Palmer, *Let Your Life Speak: Listening for the Voice of Vocation* (San Francisco: Jossey-Bass Inc., Publishers, 2000), 10.

48. Henri J. M. Nouwen, *Clowning in Rome* (Garden City, N.Y.: Doubleday, 1979), 87.

49. This question is taken from *Come Follow Me* (New York: Office for Church Life and Leadership, 1989), 13. This is an especially helpful resource for exploring vocation and call.

50. As quoted by Richard L. Morgan in *Remembering Your Story: A Guide to Spiritual Autobiography* (Nashville: Upper Room Books, 1996), 136.

51. Jack Kornfield, *A Path with Heart: A Guide Through the Perils and Promises of Spiritual Life* (New York: Bantam Books, 1993), 302-303.

52. Benedicta Ward, trans., *The Sayings of the Desert Fathers* (Kalamazoo, Michigan: Cistercian Publications, 1975), 2.

53. Dorothy Bass, ed., *Practicing Our Faith* (San Francisco: Jossey-Bass, Inc., 1997), 57-58.

54. Taken from "The Ten Commandments" (of the Nonviolent Movement), Martin Luther King, Jr., *Why We Can't Wait* (New York: Harper & Row, 1964), 61.

55. Schaper, *Sabbath Sense*, 36.

56. Whitcomb, *Feasting with God*, 142.

57. Adapted from Sidney B. Simon, Leland W. Howe, and Howard Kirschenbaum, *Values Clarification* (New York: Hart Publishing Company, Inc., 1978), 311-312.

58. Malcolm Warford, *Our Several Callings* (New York: United Church Board for Homeland Ministries, 1990), 10, 13, 19.

seven: practicing accountability

59. Julia Cameron, *Some People Say That God Is No Laughing Matter* (New York: Jeremy P. Tarcher, 2000), 64.

60. Anne Lamott, *Traveling Mercies: Some Thoughts on Faith* (New York: Pantheon, 1999), 100.

61. Flexner, ed., *The Random House Dictionary of the English Language, Second Edition, Unabridged*, 1987.

62. Macrina Wiederkehr, "Finding Balance in a Hurried World," a retreat a Schoenstatt Retreat Center, Waukesha, Wisconsin, 30-31 December 1998.

63. As quoted by Robin R. Meyers in *Morning Sun on a White Piano: Simple Pleasures and the Sacramental Life* (New York: Doubleday, 1998), 12-13.

appendix a

64. Thanks to friend and poet Nancy Dawn for inspiring me on a Moon Beach walk.

appendix b

65. Marjory Zoet Bankson, *This Is My Body: Creativity, Clay, and Change* (Philadelphia: Innisfree Press, 1993). From pages 31, 53, 86, 112, 173.

selected bibliography

Albom, Mitch. *Tuesdays with Morrie.* New York: Doubleday, 1997.

Andrews, Cicile. *The Circle of Simplicity.* New York: HarperCollins, 1997.

Bankson, Marjory Zoet. *The Call to the Soul: Six Stages of Spiritual Development.* Philadelphia: Innisfree Press, 1999.

____. *This Is My Body: Creativity, Clay, and Change.* Philadelphia: Innisfree Pres, 1993.

Bass, Dorothy C., ed. *Practicing Our Faith: A Way of Life for a Searching People.* San Francisco: Jossey-Bass, 1997.

____. *Receiving the Day: Christian Practices for Opening the Gift of Time.* San Francisco: Jossey-Bass, 2000.

Beers, Edwin. "A Life of Intercession," *Spirit Unfolding* (Winter 1999): 1-3.

Bohler, Carolyn Stahl. *Prayer on Wings: A Search for Authentic Prayer.* San Diego: LuraMedia, 1990.

Buechner, Frederick. *Wishful Thinking: A Seeker's ABC.* San Francisco: HarperSanFrancisco, 1993.

Cameron, Julia. *Some People Say that God Is No Laughing Matter.* New York: Jeremy P. Tarcher, 2000.

Campbell, Joseph with Bill Moyers, *The Power of Myth.* New York: Doubleday, 1988.

The Canticles from *The Liturgical Psalter.* Chicago: Liturgy Training Publications, 1995.

Claypool, John. *Tracks of a Fellow Struggler: How to Handle Grief.* Waco, Texas: Word Books, 1974.

Come Follow Me. New York: Office for Church Life and Leadership, 1989.

Edwards, Tilden H. *Spiritual Friend: Reclaiming the Gift of Spiritual Direction.* New York: Paulist Press, 1980.

____. *Living in the Presence: Disciplines for the Spiritual Heart.* San Francisco: Harper & Row, 1987.

____. *Sabbath Time.* Nashville: Upper Room Books, 1992.

Foster, Richard J. *Celebration of Discipline: The Path to Spiritual Growth,* revised edition. San Francisco: Harper & Row, 1998.

Fry, Timothy, O.S.B., ed. *The Rule of St. Benedict in English.* Collegeville, Minnesota: The Liturgical Press, 1992.

Ganim, Barbara, and Susan Fox. *Visual Journaling: Going Deeper Than Words.* Wheaton, Illinois: Quest Books, 1999.

Goldberg, Bonni. *Room to Write.* New York: Jeremy P. Tarcher/Putnam, 1996.

Harris, Maria. *Dance of the Spirit: The Seven Steps of Women's Spirituality.* New York: Bantam Books, 1989.

Heschel, Abraham Joshua. *The Sabbath: Its Meaning for Modern Man.* New York: Noonday Press, 1951.

King, Martin Luther, Jr. *Why We Can't Wait.* New York: Harper & Row, 1964.

Kornfield, Jack. *A Path with Heart: A Guide Through the Perils and Promises of Spiritual Life.* New York: Bantam, 1993.

Lamott, Anne. *Traveling Mercies: Some Thoughts on Faith.* New York: Pantheon, 1999.

Leder, Drew. *Games for the Soul.* New York: Hyperion, 1998.

Levertov, Denise. *Oblique Prayers.* New York: New Directions, 1984.

Meyers, Robin R. *Morning Sun on a White Piano: Simple Pleasures and the Sacramental Life.* New York: Doubleday, 1998.

Morgan, Richard L. *Remembering Your Story: A Guide to Spiritual Autobiography.* Nashville: Upper Room Books, 1996.

Moroni, Giancarlo. *My Hands Held Out to You: The Use of Body and Hands in Prayer.* Mahweh, New Jersey: Paulist Press, 1992.

Muller, Wayne. *Sabbath: Restoring the Sacred Rhythm of Rest.* New York: Bantam, 1999.

The New Century Hymnal. Cleveland: Pilgrim Press, 1995.

Nhat Hanh, Thich. *Peace Is Every Step.* New York: Bantam, 1992.

___. *Present Moment Wonderful Moment.* Berkeley: Parallax Press, 1990.

Nouwen, Henri J. M. *Clowning in Rome.* Garden City, New York: Doubleday, 1979.

Owens, Jesse with Paul G. Niemark. *Blackthink: My Life as Black Man and White Man.* New York: William Morrow and Company, Inc., 1970.

Palmer, Parker J. *Let Your Life Speak: Listening for the Voice of Vocation.* San Francisco: Jossey-Bass, Inc. 2000.

Pilgrim Hymnal. New York: The Pilgrim Press, 1986.

Redmont, Jane. *When In Doubt, Sing: Prayer in Daily Life.* New York: HarperCollinsPublishers, 1999.

Remen, Naomi Rachel. *Kitchen Table Wisdom: Stories That Heal.* New York: Riverhead Books, 1996.

Rupp, Joyce. *The Cup of Our Life: A Guide for Spiritual Growth.* Notre Dame, Indiana: Ave Maria Press, 1997.

Ryan, M. J., ed. *A Grateful Heart.* Berkeley: Conari Press, 1994.

Schaper, Donna. *Sabbath Sense: A Spiritual Antidote for the Overworked.* Philadelphia: Innisfree Press, 1997.

Schroeder, Celeste Snowbar. *Embodied Prayer: Harmonizing Body and Soul.* Liguori, Missouri: Triumph Books, 1995.

Simon, Sidney B., Leland W. Howe, and Howard Kirschenbaum. *Values Clarification.* New York: Hart Publishing Company, Inc., 1978.

Steere, Douglas V. "Intercession: Caring for Souls." *Weavings* 4, no. 2 (March/April 1989): 16-25.

Sweeney, Jon M. *Praying with Our Hands.* Woodstock, Vermont: Skylight Paths Publishing, 2000.

Thompson, Marjorie J. *Soul Feast: An Invitation to the Christian Spiritual Life.* Louisville: Westminster John Knox, 1995.

Ward, Benedicta, trans. *The Sayings of the Desert Fathers.* Kalamazoo, Michigan: Cistercian Publications, 1975.

Warford, Malcolm. *Our Several Callings.* New York: United Church Board for Homeland Ministries, 1990.

Whitcomb, Holly W. *Feasting with God: Adventures in Table Spirituality.* Cleveland: United Church Press, 1996.

Wimberly, Edward P. *Recalling Our Own Stories: Spiritual Renewal for Religious Caregivers.* San Francisco: Jossey-Bass, Inc. 1997.

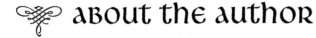 # about the author

Holly Wilson Whitcomb has been a pastor and clergywoman in the United Church of Christ since her graduation from Yale Divinity School in 1978, and has served churches in Connecticut, Iowa, and Wisconsin. She is also a graduate of the two-year training program for spiritual directors at the Shalem Institute for Spiritual Formation in Bethesda, Maryland. As the Director of Kettlewood Retreats, Holly is a retreat leader and spiritual director who travels to churches, retreat houses, and conference centers across the country. She is also a jewelry-maker who has donated a number of her pieces to charity auctions and who often incorporates "art as meditation" into her retreats. Holly is the author of numerous articles on spirituality as well as the book *Feasting with God*. She lives in a suburb of Milwaukee, Wisconsin with her husband John, and their two children, David and Kate.

You may contact Holly Whitcomb by calling the Kettlewood Retreats Office at (262) 784-5593 or by sending e-mail to: hwhitcomb@wi.rr.com.

Breinigsville, PA USA
22 December 2009
229688BV00003B/14/P